An Essay on Irish Bulls

CLASSICS OF IRISH HISTORY
General Editor: Tom Garvin

Original publication dates of reprinted titles are given in brackets

P. S. O'Hegarty, *The Victory of Sinn Féin* (1924)
Walter McDonald, *Some Ethical Questions of Peace and War* (1919)
Joseph Johnston, *Civil War in Ulster* (1913)
James Mullin, *The Story of a Toiler's Life* (1921)
Robert Brennan, *Ireland Standing Firm* and *Eamon de Valera* (1958)
Mossie Harnett, *Victory and Woe: The West Limerick
Brigade in the War of Independence*
Padraig de Burca and John F. Boyle, *Free State or Republic?
Pen Pictures of the Historic Treaty Session of Dáil Éireann* (1922)
Arthur Clery, *The Idea of a Nation* (1907)
Standish James O'Grady, *To the Leaders of Our Working People*
Michael Davitt, *Jottings in Solitary*
Oliver MacDonagh, *Ireland: The Union and its Aftermath* (1977)
Thomas Fennell, *The Royal Irish Constabulary: A History and Personal Memoir*
Arthur Griffith, *The Resurrection of Hungary* (1918)
William McComb, *The Repealer Repulsed* (1841)
George Moore, *Parnell and His Island* (1887)
Charlotte Elizabeth Tonna, *Irish Recollections* (1841/47 as *Personal Recollections*)
Standish James O'Grady, *Sun and Wind*
John Sarsfield Casey, *The Galtee Boy: A Fenian Prison Narrative*
William and Mary Ann Hanbidge,
Memories of West Wicklow: 1813–1939 (1939)
A. P. A. O'Gara, *The Green Republic* (1902)
William Cooke Taylor, *Reminiscences of Daniel O'Connell* (1847)
William Bruce and Henry Joy, *Belfast Politics* (1794)
Annie O'Donnell, *Your Fondest Annie*
Joseph Keating, *My Struggle for Life* (1916)
John Mitchel, *The Last Conquest of Ireland (Perhaps)* (1858/9)
Harold Begbie, *The Lady Next Door* (1914)
Eugene Davis, *Souvenirs of Footprints Over Europe* (1889)
Maria Edgeworth, *An Essay on Irish Bulls* (1802)
D. P. Moran, *The Philosophy of Irish Ireland* (1898–1900)
T. M. Kettle, *The Open Secret of Ireland* (1912)

An Essay on Irish Bulls

✦

MARIA EDGEWORTH

with an introduction by Jane Desmarais
edited by Jane Desmarais
and Marilyn Butler

UNIVERSITY COLLEGE DUBLIN PRESS
Preas Choláiste Ollscoile Bhaile Átha Cliath

First published 1802
Editorial material © Jane Desmarais and Marilyn Butler
text © Pickering & Chatto Ltd.
Hardback published by Pickering & Chatto Ltd. 1999
This edition first published by University College Dublin Press, 2006
Introduction © Jane Desmarais 2006

ISBN 978-1-904558-75-0
ISSN 1393-6883

University College Dublin Press
86 St Stephen's Green
Dublin 2
Ireland
www.ucdpress.ie

All rights reserved. No part of this publication
may be reproduced, stored in a retrieval system,
or transmitted in any form or by any means,
electronic, photocopying, recording or
otherwise without the prior written
permission of the publisher

Cataloguing in Publication data
available from the British Library

Typeset in France in Ehrhardt by Elaine Burberry
Text design by Lyn Davies, Frome, Somerset, England
Printed in England on acid-free paper by
Athenaeum Press Ltd., Gateshead, Tyne & Wear

CONTENTS

Note on the Text		*vi*
INTRODUCTION *by Jane Desmarais*		*vii*

AN ESSAY ON IRISH BULLS

	Introduction	*3*
I	Originality of Irish Bulls Examined	*6*
II	Irish Newspapers	*12*
III	The Criminal Law of Bulls and Blunders	*21*
IV	Little Dominick	*26*
V	The Bliss of Ignorance	*36*
VI	'Thoughts that Breathe and Words that Burn'	*42*
VII	Practical Bulls	*48*
VIII	The Dublin Shoeblack	*53*
IX	The Hibernian Mendicant	*62*
X	Irish Wit and Eloquence	*68*
XI	The Brogue	*77*
XII	Bath Coach Conversation	*82*
XIII	Bath Coach Conversation	*91*
XIV	The Irish Incognito	*95*
	Conclusion	*120*
	Editors' notes	*124*

Note on the Text

The text of *Irish Bulls* has been typeset from Volume 1 of the Pickering & Chatto edition of *The Novels and Selected Works of Maria Edgeworth* (12 vols, 1999), edited by Jane Desmarais, Tim McLoughlin and Marilyn Butler. Published first in 1802, re-editions of *An Essay on Irish Bulls* appeared in 1808 and 1832 (the *Collected Works* edition); of these, the third edition of 1832 is taken as the significant and standard, as it is based on the 1808 text which was purposefully revised and shortened by the authors. The text here has been altered very little, with only very minor modifications made to spelling and punctuation, and it is published without variants. The footnotes are Maria Edgeworth's, while the endnotes are the responsibility of the editors.

INTRODUCTION
Jane Desmarais

'what we call the Irish Brogue is no sooner discovered, than it makes the deliverer, in the last degree, ridiculous and despised; and from such a mouth, an Englishman expects nothing but bulls, blunders, and follies. Neither does it avail whether the censure be reasonable or not, since the fact is always so.'[1]

An Essay on Irish Bulls was first published in 1802 for five shillings as a kind of common-place book devoted to showing the English public the wit and repartee of the lower Irish classes. Originally devised by Maria's father, Richard Lovell Edgeworth, and drawing on issues of language and rhetoric that go back to the ancient world, *Irish Bulls* is an informal philosophic dialogue on the nature of bulls (logical absurdities and incongruities) and jokes and jests in general. It was published at the time of the Union, and the overarching theme of the essay is the relationship between national identity and cultural character, its aim to show that the practice of making bulls is no more peculiar to the Irish than to any other people. Its subject is, in short, prejudice articulated through humour. As Marilyn Butler puts it, 'The witty, skilful use of language by the Irish indicates that they have the education and ability to take their place in a modern commercial nation, while the so-called Irish Bull is exposed as an ungenerous fiction deployed by its main users, the English of all ranks, to deny the Irish equality on the grounds of their alleged "imbecility".[2]

The underlying principle of *Irish Bulls* is that bulls are not solely imputable to the Irish and that Hibernian English is as rich and revealing of cultural attitudes as other English dialects, including Cockney, Somerset, Lancashire, Yorkshire, Welsh and Scots. Chapter VIII describes the eloquent and colourful street slang of Dublin, for example. Entitled 'The Dublin Shoeblack', it details the case of a shoeblack on trial for murder. The theme of this episode, as of the others featuring individuals ('Little Dominick' – chapter IV; 'The Hibernian Mendicant', chapter IX; and 'The Irish Incognito'– chapter XIV) is the fertility of the Irish imagination and their manipulation of language, and the authors gloss their pedantry with a measure of playful irony:

> *Billy, says I, will you sky a copper?*
>
> A copper! genus pro specie! the generic name of copper of the base individual halfpenny.
>
> *Sky a copper.*
>
> To sky is a new verb, which none but a master hand could have coined: a more splendid metonymy could not be applied upon a more trivial occasion: the lofty idea of raising a metal to the skies is substituted for the mean thought of tossing up a halfpenny. Our orator compresses his hyperbole into a single word. Thus the mind is prevented from dwelling long enough upon the figure to perceive its enormity. This is the perfection of the art. (p. 55)

To point up the rhetorical sophistication of Hibernian English was, in effect, to overturn a longstanding view of the Irish, which saw them as wild and savage. This view can be traced back to medieval times,[3] but as Mitzi Myers argues in her essay 'Goring John Bull:

Introduction

Maria Edgeworth's Hibernian High Jinks versus the Imperialist Imaginary' (1995), the bull or blunder was a seventeenth-century colonialist conception which invariably masked a fear of the Other.[4] Restoration drama was full of jokes against the Irish, but it was not until the eighteenth century, however, that the bull was identified as stereotypically Irish. A book specifically about Irish bulls was an idea first mooted by Jonathan Swift in a letter to Lord Bathurst of 1730, in which he proposed to write a satirical work on the English and their jokes about the 'Irish bull' or blunder.[5] The Edgeworths were familiar with this letter, and it inspired their search for bulls during the late 1790s. In collecting examples of bulls from Ireland, England, Wales, Scotland, and elsewhere, their aim was not to lampoon the English stereotyping of the Irish (à la Swift) but to evoke the subtle linguistic reciprocities between the English and Irish, and, more generally, the shifting, fluid nature of national identity. Myers makes this point well: England's depiction of Ireland in the essay is also – covertly – a depiction of England.[6]

It was R. L. Edgeworth who passed the idea for a book on Irish bulls to his daughter, and though a studious collation of bulls begins in the late 1790s, the writing of the essay gets under way a few years later in 1801–2. This was a very productive period for both Maria and her father. Maria began collecting bulls when she was a teenager, but it was not until she started to publish regularly in the late 1790s that she collated and sourced them for the purposes of writing a coherent essay on their significance.[7] Encouraged by her father to make accurate and precise notes about speech she had overheard and books she had read, Maria began to hunt for verbal blunders in earnest. In 1801, she asked her step-aunt, Harriet Beaufort, to collect English bulls for her. Maria wrote, 'One English bull is worth ten Irish for my purpose.'[8] R. L. Edgeworth was a guiding presence and voice throughout the conception and execution of *Irish Bulls*. Much of the material on ancient languages and Irish speech, especially in chapters VIII and X, can be traced to him. But, in spite of the scholarly speculation which continues to interrogate his presence in Maria's writings generally, the essay is understood to be a collaborative effort, with Maria as the principal author. She herself declared, 'No book was ever written more completely in partnership'.[9]

The years 1795–1817 were phenomenally productive for Maria; they coincided with the cataclysmic upheaval of the Irish Rebellion of 1798, Ireland's parliamentary Union with England (1800–1), and the Peace of Amiens (1802–3). The Edgeworths were caught up in the military revolt in Ireland which disrupted life for both landlord and tenant. Maria's father took up arms to defend Longford from the French and they were driven from their home to take shelter at a nearby inn. In this context it appears that *Irish Bulls* reflects contemporary political controversies, containing, as it does, a challenge to the anti-Catholic polemic of the parliamentarian, Sir Richard Musgrave. His *Memoirs of the Various Rebellions in Ireland, 1641, 1688, 1798* (Dublin, 1801) traced the roots of the civil wars back to conspiracies and treacheries by Catholic priests. In *Irish Bulls*, Musgrave's anti-Catholicism is held up for correction. At the end of chapter II, the English commander General Lake is described as hunting 'the human biped as fair game' (p. 20).

An Essay on Irish Bulls is not an overtly political text, but in the asides and in the footnotes a liberal and pro-Catholic agenda is evident. By insisting on the notion of the Irish bull, the English fail to recognise their own sense of inferiority, but in the essay, the English are cleverly made to have a degree of insight. In chapter XII, 'Bath Coach Conversation', for example, the Englishman asserts, 'bulls are not peculiar to Ireland. I have been informed by a person of unquestionable authority, that there is a town in Germany, Hirschau in the upper Palatinate, where the inhabitants are famous for making bulls.' (p. 85) In the closing passage of the Conclusion, the authors make a more direct political comment: 'Whatever might have been the policy of the English nation towards Ireland whilst she was a separate kingdom, since the union it can no longer be her wish to depreciate the talents or ridicule the language of the Hibernians.' (p. 123)

The main subject of the essay, however, is the humour found in speech. Countless examples of Irish expressiveness and their equivalent in English, Welsh, and Scots form the material of the central chapters. Rather than make a point about English prejudice overtly in the text, the authors rely on the self-evidence of the reported speech and the irony of encounters between individuals of different nationalities to make political points. The recurrent theme is the 'infinite variety' of the bull, its universal cultural significance, and above all its elusiveness: 'The essence of an Irish bull must be of the most ethereal nature, for notwithstanding the most indefatigable research, it has hitherto escaped from analysis.' (p. 5)

An Essay on Irish Bulls is an important primary text for all students of literature and cultural history. Not only does it reflect the contemporary social and political preoccupations of the Anglo-Irish at the turn of the nineteenth century, particularly in relation to the strain put on both nations by the Union and reform for Catholic Emancipation, but it is an important document about that most elusive of subjects – verbal humour. The Edgeworths join a very short but eminent line of philosophers of the joke. Like such distinguished later commentators on humour – Bergson, Meredith, Freud – they attempt to explain humour and jokes as devices of saying what is difficult to say or what is unsayable. Viewed in this context, the Edgeworths attempt to make the Irish bull speak about a long history of prejudice and divisive conflict. As Ted Cohen has argued in *Jokes: Philosophical Thoughts on Joking Matters* (1999), racism and nationalism thrive on a currency of jokes, and humour is most often the way in which different peoples are made to identify with one another.[10] Swift may have recognised this in 1730, but the Edgeworths were the first to articulate the complexity of relations between Ireland and England through jokes and witticisms. Without satirising or lampooning their target, they brilliantly reveal the flaws in English perceptions about the Irish bull and demonstrate the ways in which the Irish were made and played at being the colonial underdog.

Irish Bulls was published in five editions, in 1802, 1803, 1808, 1815 and 1823, and it was twice published as a single volume in America in 1803, by Duane (Philadelphia) and Swaine (New York). This edition of *Irish Bulls* is the first stand-alone edition to be published since the nineteenth century, and it is based on the text of the 1832 *Collected Edition*. The 1832 edition (essentially the revised and shortened third edition of 1808) is the standard text and it is used in the 12-volume *Novels and Selected Works of Maria Edgeworth*, Pickering & Chatto, 1999.[11] In the Advertisement to the third edition of 1808, Maria and her father write: 'When authors receive any degree of encouragement from the public, it should incite them to increasing diligence: a third edition of this Essay on Irish Bulls has been called for, and the authors of this Essay have taken pains to correct and *shorten* it.' In fact, the authors cut the essay by a fifth.[12] It was received with mixed reviews. Sydney Smith in the *Edinburgh Review* of July 1803 announced it as a 'rambling, scrambling book'[13] and was harsh about 'Mr Edgeworth', who he suspected was the principal author:[14]

> The essay on bulls is written much with the same mind and in the same manner, as a school-boy takes a walk: He moves on for ten yards on a straight road, with surprising perseverance; then sets out after a butterfly, looks for a bird's nest, or jumps backwards and forwards over a ditch. In the same manner, this nimble and progressive gentleman is away after every object which crosses his mind.... He is fuddled with

animal spirits, giddy with constitutional joy; in such a state he must have written on or burst.[15]

Smith is more than complimentary, however, on the Edgeworths' portrayal of the Irish character, declaring the 'imitation of the Irish manner' to be 'first-rate':[16]

> Whether the Irish make more bulls than their neighbours, is, as we have before remarked, not a point of much importance; but it is of considerable importance, that the character of a nation should not be degraded; and Mr Edgeworth has great merit in his benevolent intention of doing justice to the excellent qualities of the Irish. It is not possible to read his book, without feeling a strong and a new disposition in their favour.[17]

On the subject of Irish wit and eloquence (the title of chapter X), the Edgeworths are at their best, and they reveal an appreciative sensitivity to their subject. In an attempt to 'conciliate both countries' (p.123) and to diffuse a more realistic picture of the Irish at a time of considerable political tension between the two countries, the authors take care to bring out the native intelligence behind verbal incongruity. In chapter X, for example, they compare the lower Irish with the Classical poets in their ingenious similes, claiming that 'Innumerable instances might be quoted of the Hibernian genius' (p. 69). What the essay does essentially is to explore the ingenuity of a creative principle at work in Irish fiction from the time of Swift to the present day. The indefinability of the bull, as the essay proves, is part of its comical impact and genius, and by attempting to circumscribe it, the Edgeworths have to admit that it is uncircumscribable. In the Introduction they make a dual claim that by 'ascertaining what it is not, we may discover what it is' (p. 5). In linguistic terms, we never find the bull pinned down, but politically, the message is clear: the English idea of a bull is a deliberate misconception; a bull is not an inferior mode of speech belonging to the Irish only, but can be found in a range of other languages and dialects in the Union and elsewhere.

BIOGRAPHY

Maria Edgeworth was born at the home of her maternal grandfather, Black Bourton in Oxfordshire, on 1 January 1768. She was the third of five children born of Richard Lovell Edgeworth (1744–1817) and Anna Maria Elers (1743–73). As the Oxford DNB entry puts it, R. L. Edgeworth 'was both libidinous and abstracted',[18] marrying four times and siring 22 children. Maria's mother died in March 1773, and in July of the same year her father re-married Honora Sneyd of Lichfield (1751–80). When Honora died in 1780, R. L. Edgeworth married her sister, Elizabeth (1753–97), within the year. When she died in 1797, he met Frances Anne Beaufort (1769–1867) and they married in 1798 and had six children. Maria had an unhappy childhood. She was intelligent and restless, and she felt neglected by her father, who was continuously busy with his main interests in politics, science and education.

After Maria's mother died, the family moved in 1782 to her father's estate in Edgeworthstown, County Longford, but as Maria and her brother Richard proved rather difficult children, they were sent to English boarding schools in 1775. Maria attended Madame Lattafière's[19] school in Derby until 1780 studying, among other subjects, dancing and French, and then went to Mrs Devis's school in Upper Wimpole Street, London. She was an energetic storyteller and a voracious reader, and kept her peers entertained in the dormitories with her stories. As the eldest daughter, Maria became very close to her father, who coached her in writing and primed her early for a career in publishing. He was a profound intellectual and editorial influence on her work, and encouraged her to employ her literary talents in giving a disinterested and precise account of the world around her. Maria began writing at school, but on her return to Ireland spent her teenage years and her twenties looking after her younger siblings, educating them and helping manage the dilapidated family estate. In intellectual terms, she followed in the footsteps of her father. She was a member of the Lunar Society (like her father) and became a scientific educationist, writing tales and lessons for children. By 1801, as Butler has noted, Maria was 'virtually a one-woman library for parents teaching at home'.[20] The first edition of *Letters for Literary Ladies* was published in 1795, and in 1796 three volumes of *The Parent's Assistant: or Stories for Children* appeared. Maria's most influential work of this period, however, was *Practical Education*, published with her father in two volumes in 1798. This book established her reputation across Europe and was reprinted many times.[21]

From 1802, Maria began her travels to the Continent, accompanied by her father, meeting scholars, philosophers and writers. In 1802, they visited Paris, and immediately enjoyed acclaim on account of *Practical Education*, co-authored with her father and published in two volumes. They were besieged with invitations.[22] Among those they met were the English inventor James Watt, the young English nobleman Henry Petty and his former tutor and utilitarian, Etienne Dumont, whom she met in London in 1813 and with whom she corresponded on the subjects of education and penology. Dumont became for the Edgeworths an intellectual conduit between Ireland, England and France. In 1803, Maria made a short trip to Edinburgh, staying with Dugald Stewart, a Scottish empiricist and Professor of Moral Philosophy, who had taught her father. The intellectual culture of Edinburgh and Glasgow was important to both Maria and her father, but Paris influenced her more. She read widely in French, using her experience of fashionable life there for her tales. She made many visits to London, beginning in 1813, where she was received enthusiastically in literary and intellectual circles; however, travelling only confirmed for her the importance of family life in Edgeworthstown.

Maria's fame in Europe quickly spread through journals and translations of her work. She continued to write children's stories, educational works, fiction and non-fiction,[23] but from 1800 she was increasingly attracted to documenting Irish culture and was deeply influenced by the social and political changes in her adopted country. Her novels (*Castle Rackrent* (1800), *Ennui* (1809), *The Absentee* (1812) and *Ormond* (1817)) reflect her concern for estate business, in particular the abuses of landlordism and the lives and customs of the tenants. As well as documenting social realities, these tales draw extensively on anecdotes from the Edgeworth family, extending back to Maria's grandfather, Richard Edgeworth (1701–70). *Ennui* and *The Absentee* were highly acclaimed by the critics and confirmed her reputation as a realist writer. Maria did not write only about Ireland. Many of her tales are set in England, but often include characters from Ireland, Scotland and France. These tales are about fashionable life, its private and the public aspects. *Belinda* was published in 1801, *Patronage* (her longest novel) in 1814, and *Helen* in 1834. Unlike most of her tales, which adapt the form of the English and French genres of the novella or philosophic tale, these works were of standard novel length. In 1817, following the death of her father, Maria's literary production slowed, as she took over the management of the family estate with her stepmother. Maria published two more books, *Harry and Lucy Concluded* (1825) and *Helen* (1834). She spent her last years raising American money for victims of the Irish Famine and died at home in Edgeworthstown on 22 May 1849.

Introduction

A PHILOSOPHICAL SPECTATRESS

In spite of her widening circle of friends and intellectual acquaintances, Maria's main inspiration for writing continued to be her experience of Ireland, its contemporary culture and long, vivid history. In Edgeworthstown she lived among the landed gentry with a keen eye for the local life, which she would observe on her tours round the estate. The Irish tenants and peasants were a rich source for her fictional writings, and she and her father built an extensive archive of their phrases, anecdotes and manners. This meticulously recorded archive formed the material for *Irish Bulls*. In the essay, the authors draw attention to their methodology, emphasising that all but a few of the anecdotes included in *Irish Bulls* were given to them personally: 'The examples we have cited are taken from real life, and given without alteration or embellishment' (p. 76). Their aim was to remain unobtrusive and scientific in their reporting and presentation of Irish speech, and so dialogues are sometimes left to stand alone, without critical commentary. In the footnote at the end of chapter X, for example, which contains a dispute between a poor widow and a landlord, the authors reassure the reader by saying that 'This was written down a few minutes after it had been spoken.' (p. 76)[24]

Keenness and accuracy of observation are characteristics of Maria's writing. She was a didactic and realist writer whose aim was to document life. In her correspondence with Etienne Dumont, she describes her tendency to concentrate on local detail. Acknowledging the superior knowledge of the world of the male members of her family, she comments on the necessity of observing closely:

> I don't think I was much if at all improved as a writer, by a winter in Paris, or by a visit to Edinburgh or Dublin. The views of characters in society are too confined & transitory. There is not time to see justly – &

the objects are too near. *Travellers* seldom from such cursory observations represent *manners* much less *motives* faithfully. I have, I think, gained more as a writer by hearing & comparing these presentations of persons of sense & of *fools* who have furnished Maria with facts [or] observations according to their various ways of seeing and feeling. I have a father & brothers & friends who continually supply Maria with variety from that *world* in which I don't live, or wish to live.[25]

She continues to describe herself modestly as a person distracted by seemingly inconsequential trifles:

If I were merely a writer I might perhaps see better & see only as a writer in society, but a number of different feelings – many of them most trifling & foolish perhaps, some for the friends who are with Maria, some for myself disturb my spirit of observation, & unfit Maria for a *philosophical spectatress* in the world. For instance, I might at a dinner with the grandest or wittiest people in London be totally absorbed in considering whether the bones in the fish my father was eating would choak him or not, or (more foolishly) – whether my mothers cap became her, or whether the persons who might be complimenting me thought me idiot, or authoress enough to believe them *occupied de la lettre*.[26]

A 'philosophical spectatress' describes Maria well. She was a writer profoundly influenced by the late-Enlightenment values of detachment and objectivity, inherited from the scientific and progressive principles of her father. Maria was as interested in ideas as in people and places. Though her primary concern was to portray character, her fiction managed to encompass the wider cultural-political world in which these people lived. In many ways, she was a writer who resisted neat categorisation, and *Irish Bulls* is a pivotal work in this respect. One of the difficulties scholars have expressed with the essay is its allusiveness and erudition. Part of this problem may be owing to the collaborative nature of the text. The extent to which her father contributed his voice and ideas is a subject of much debate. In her informative essay, 'Goring John Bull', Mitzi Myers looks at the problematical issue of voice in Edgeworth from a postmodern perspective, describing *Irish Bulls* as both a typical and transitional work in the Edgeworth canon:

> [*Irish Bulls* is a] parodic text that destabilises the models of gendered authorship, literary genre, national identity, and critical pedophobia which have effected their author's canonical displacement. Edgeworth's fascination with identity as fashioned through language, her playfulness with linguistic codes and systems of representation, her foregrounding of dialogic form and domestic anecdote, and her peculiar mix of the demotic and allusively learned are signature traits already evident in her adolescent letters.[27]

As a late-Enlightenment woman writer working in the early Romantic period, Maria is an interstitial figure, who, as Clíona Ó Gallchoir has argued in her book, *Maria Edgeworth: Women, Enlightenment and Nation* (2005), often suffers from marginalisation by literary scholars on the basis that she is out of step with her times: 'seemingly anomalous as an Enlightenment writer in a Romantic age', she writes, '[Maria] is positioned on the wrong side of a historical, political, philosophic and aesthetic divide'.[28] *Irish Bulls* proves this otherwise, showing Maria to be very much in step with her times and able to bring her rational and erudite perspective to bear on a subject that is both comic and serious.

An Essay on Irish Bulls

Notes to Introduction

My thanks to Catherine Fuller at the Bentham Project, University College London for her help with the Dumont correspondence, to Bill Mc Cormack for putting me on the track of bulls in the first place, and to Barbara Mennell at UCD Press.

1 Jonathan Swift, 'On Barbarous Denominations in Ireland', *The Prose Works of Jonathan Swift*, ed. Herbert Davis, 14 vols (Oxford: Blackwell, 1957), IV, p. 281.

2 See the Introductory Note to the Pickering & Chatto edition of *The Novels and Selected Works of Maria Edgeworth*, 12 vols (1999), I, p. xxii.

3 See W. J. Lawrence, *Speeding Up Shakespeare: Studies of the Bygone Theatre and Drama* (London: Argonaut Press, 1937); J. O. Bartley, 'Bulls and Bog Witticisms', *Irish Book Lover* XXX (Nov. 1947), pp. 59–62; J. O. Bartley, *Teague, Shenkin, and Sawney: Being an Historical Study of the Earliest Irish, Welsh, and Scottish Characters in English Plays* (Cork: Cork UP, 1954), chapter 11; Kathleen Rabl, 'Taming the "Wild Irish" in English Renaissance Drama', in *Literary Interrelations: Ireland, England, and the World*, vol. 3: *National Images and Stereotypes*, ed. Wolfgang Zach and Heinz Kosok (Tübingen: Narr, 1987), pp. 47–75; Annelise Truninger, *Paddy and the Paycock: A Study of the Stage Irishman from Shakespeare to O'Casey* (Bern: Francke, 1976); D. W. Hayton, 'From Barbarian to Burlesque: English Images of the Irish *c.*1660–1750', *Journal of Economic and Social History* XV (1988), pp. 5–31; Cóilín Owens, 'Irish Bulls in *Castle Rackrent*', in *Family Chronicles: Maria Edgeworth's 'Castle Rackrent'*, ed. Cóilín Owens (Dublin: Wolfhound Press; Totowa, NJ: Barnes & Noble, 1987), pp. 70–8; Joseph Th. Leerssen, *Mere Irish and Fíor-Ghael: Studies in the Idea of Irish Nationality, Its Development, and Literary Expression Prior to the Nineteenth Century*, Utrecht Publications in General and Comparative Literature, vol. 22 (Amsterdam: John Benjamin, 1986), chapter 3.

4 'the imperialist cannot laugh benevolently at the native's inherent verbal ineptitude if he is too scared' (see Mitzi Myers, 'Goring John Bull: Maria Edgeworth's Hibernian High Jinks versus the Imperialist Imaginary', in *Cutting Edges: Postmodern Critical Essays on Eighteenth-century Satire*, ed. James E. Gill (Knoxville: University of Tennessee Press, 1995), pp. 367–94: p. 372.

5 Swift to Lord Bathurst, October 1730; ed. Harold Williams, *Swift's Correspondence*, 5 vols. (Oxford: Clarendon Press, 1963), III, p. 411: 'there must be a long Introduction proving the native Irish rabble to have a better tact for

Wit than the English, for which philosophical causes shall be assigned and many instances produced'.

6 Myers, 'Goring John Bull', p. 373.

7 The Edgeworths' sources included dictionaries, grammars, anthologies, encyclopaedias, 'synonymies' and jestbooks; for more detail see M. Butler's 'Introductory Note' in *The Novels and Selected Works of Maria Edgeworth*, I, pp. xvii–xxx.

8 Maria Edgeworth to SR, n.d. [Oct 1797]; M. Butler, *Maria Edgeworth: A Literary Biography* (Oxford, 1972), p. 245; quoted in the 'Introductory Note', *The Novels and Selected Works of Maria Edgeworth*, I, p. xvi.

9 [Maria Edgeworth], *Memoirs of Richard Lovell Edgeworth*, 2 vols (London: R. Miles, 1820), II, p. 336.

10 See Ted Cohen, *Jokes: Philosophical Thoughts on Joking Matters* (Chicago: Chicago UP, 1999), and the passage quoted in Adam Phillips's review of Cohen's book:

> When we laugh at the same thing, that is a very special occasion. It is already noteworthy that we laugh at all, at anything, and that we laugh all alone. That we do it together is the satisfaction of a deep, human longing, the realization of a desperate hope. It is the hope that we are enough like one another to sense one another, to be able to live together.

Quoted by Adam Phillips in 'Jokes Apart', in *Promises, Promises: Essays on Literature and Psychoanalysis* (London: Faber, 2000), p. 352.

11 See pp. 69–153 (text) and 320–42 (endnotes) of the Pickering & Chatto edition.

12 For a detailed summary of the changes made to the essay in 1803 and 1808, see the textual variants in Vol. 1 of the Pickering & Chatto edition of *The Novels and Selected Works of Maria Edgeworth*, pp. 369–97.

13 [Sydney Smith], *Edinburgh Review* II (July 1803), pp. 398–402: p. 398.

14 'we are strongly inclined to suspect that the male contributions exceed the female, in a very great degree' (ibid.).

15 Ibid.

16 Ibid., p. 402.

17 Ibid., p. 401.

18 See W. J. Mc Cormack's article 'Maria Edgeworth (1768–1849)' in the *Oxford Dictionary of Biography* (www.oxforddnb.com).

19 Edgeworth scholars spell this name differently: Lattafière (favoured by W. J. Mc Cormack et al.) is preferred here, but other sources render the spelling Latuffiere.

20 'Introductory Note' to *The Novels and Selected Works of Maria Edgeworth*, I, p. xix.

21 For bibliographical details, see the entry on Maria Edgeworth in *The Cambridge Bibliography of English Literature*, 3rd edn., vol. 4, 1800–1900 (Cambridge: CUP, 1999), pp. 901–7.

22 Details of this are given in Jefferson P. Selth, *Firm Heart and Capacious Mind* (Lanham, MD: University of America Press, 1997), p. 123.

23 See Maria's *Moral Tales* (1801); *Popular Tales* (1804); and the *Early Lessons* series, from 1801, continued at irregular intervals (*Harry and Lucy Continued*, 2 vols, 1814; *Rosamund: A Sequel*, 2 vols, 1821; *Frank: A Sequel*, 3 vols, 1822; *Harry and Lucy Concluded*, 4 vols, 1825).

24 Marilyn Butler has commented that the methodology of *Irish Bulls* affected subsequent publications. In *Maria Edgeworth: A Literary Biography*, she writes that 'As a process the Edgeworths' habit of collecting speech-specimens was careful, fairly systematic, and carried out for the purposes of science, not of literature. Because their material was intrinsically so lively, it was to be the richest ingredient in the Irish tales, although never "made over", as it were, into fiction' (Oxford: OUP, 1972, p. 363).

25 Letter to Etienne Dumont, 9 July 1811 [Bibliothèque Publique et Universitaire, Geneva, Dumont MSS, 33/II, fos. 52–5].

26 Ibid.

27 Myers, 'Goring John Bull, p. 367.

28 Clíona Ó Gallchoir, *Maria Edgeworth: Women, Enlightenment and Nation* (Dublin: UCD Press, 2005), p. 1.

An Essay on Irish Bulls

Introduction

What mortal, what fashionable mortal, is there who has not, in the midst of a formidable circle, been reduced to the embarrassment of having nothing to say? Who is there that has not felt those oppressive fits of silence which ensue after the weather, and the fashions, and the politics, and the scandal, and all the common-place topics of the day have been utterly exhausted? Who is there that, at such a time, has not tried in vain to call up an idea, and found that *none would come when they did call*,[1] or that all that came were impertinent, and must be rejected, some as too grave, others too gay, some too vulgar, some too refined for the hearers, some relating to persons, others to circumstances that must not be mentioned? Not one will do! and all this time the silence lasts, and the difficulty of breaking it increases every instant in an incalculable proportion.

Let it be some comfort to those whose polite sensibility has laboured under such distress to be assured, that they need never henceforward fear to be reduced to similar dilemmas. They may be ensured for ever against such dangers at the slight premium and upon the easy condition of perusing the following little volume. It will satisfy them that there is a subject which still affords inexhausted and inexhaustible sources of conversation, suited to all tastes, all ranks, all individuals, democratic, aristocratic, commercial, or philosophic; suited to every company which can be combined, purposely or fortuitously, in this great metropolis, or in any of the most remote parts of England, Wales, or Scotland. There is a subject which dilates the heart of every true Briton, which relaxes his muscles, however rigid, to a smile, –which opens his lips, however closed, to conversation. There is a subject 'which frets another's spleen to cure our own,'[2] and which makes even the angelic part of the creation *laugh themselves mortal*.[3] For who can forbear to laugh at the bare idea of an Irish bull?

Nor let any one apprehend that this subject can ever become trite and vulgar. Custom cannot stale its infinite variety.[4] It is in the main obvious, and palpable enough for every common understanding; yet it leads to disquisitions of exquisite subtlety, it branches into innumerable ramifications, and involves consequences of surprising importance; it may exercise the ingenuity of the subtlest wit, the fancy of the oddest humorist, the imagination of the finest poet, and the judgment of the most profound metaphysician. Moreover, this happy subject is enveloped in all that doubt and confusion which are so favourable to the reputation of disputants, and which secures the glorious possibility of talking incessantly, without being stopped short by a definition or a demonstration. For much as we have all heard and talked of Irish bulls, it has never yet been decided what it is that constitutes a bull. *Incongruity of ideas*, says one. But this supposition touches too closely upon the definition of wit, which, according to the best authorities, Locke, Burke, and Stewart,[5] consists in an unexpected assemblage of ideas, apparently discordant, but in which some point of resemblance or aptitude is suddenly discovered.

Then, perhaps, says another, the essence of a bull lies in *confusion of ideas*. This sounds plausible in theory, but it will not apply in practice; for confusion of ideas is common to both countries: for instance, was there not some slight confusion of ideas in the mind of that English student, who, when he was asked what progress he had made in the study of medicine, replied, 'I hope I shall soon be qualified to be a physician, for I think I am now able to cure a child?'[6]

To amend our bill, suppose we insert the word laughable, and say that *a laughable confusion of ideas* constitutes a bull. But have we not a laughable confusion of ideas in our English poet Blackmore's famous lines in Prince Arthur? –

> 'A painted vest prince Vortigern had on,
> Which from a naked Pict his grandsire won.'[7]

We are sensible that, to many people, the most vulgar Irish bull would appear more laughable merely from its being Irish, – therefore we cannot make the propensity to laughter in one man the criterion of what is ridiculous in another; though we have a precedent for this mode of judging in the laws of England, which are allowed to be the perfection of human reason. If a man swear that his neighbour has put him in bodily fear, he may have the cause of his terror sent to gaol; thus the feelings of the plaintiff become the measure of the defendant's guilt. As we cannot extend this convenient principle to all matters of taste, and all subjects of risibility, we are still compelled to acknowledge that no accurate definition of a bull has yet been given. The essence of an Irish bull must be of the most ethereal nature, for notwithstanding the most indefatigable research, it has hitherto escaped from analysis. The crucible always breaks in the long-expected moment of projection:[8] we have nevertheless the courage to recommence the process in a new mode. Perhaps by ascertaining what it is not, we may at last discover what it is: we must distinguish the genuine from the spurious, the original from all imitations, the indigenous from the exotic; in short, it must be determined in what an Irish bull essentially differs from a blunder, or in what Irish blunders specifically differ from English blunders, and from those of all other nations. To elucidate these points, or to prove to the satisfaction of all competent judges that they are beyond the reach of the human understanding, is the object of the following *Essay concerning the Nature of Bulls and Blunders.*

Chapter I

Originality of Irish Bulls Examined

The difficulty of selecting from the vulgar herd of Irish bulls one that shall be entitled to the prize, from the united merits of pre-eminent absurdity, and indisputable originality, is greater than hasty judges may imagine. Many bulls, reputed to be bred and born in Ireland, are of foreign extraction; and many more, supposed to be unrivalled in their kind, may be matched in all their capital *points*: for instance, there is not a more celebrated bull than Paddy Blake's. When Paddy heard an English gentleman speaking of the fine echo at the lake of Killarney, which repeats the sound forty times, he very promptly observed, 'Faith, that's nothing at all to the echo in my father's garden, in the county of Galway: if you say to it, "How do you do, Paddy Blake?" it will answer, "Pretty well, I thank you, sir."'[9]

Now this echo of Paddy Blake's, which has long been the admiration of the world, is not a prodigy *unique* in its kind; it can be matched by one recorded in the immortal works of the great lord Verulam.*

'I remember well,' says this father of philosophy, 'that when I went to the echo at port Charenton, there was an old Parisian that took it to be the work of spirits, and of good spirits, "for," said he, "call Satan, and the echo will not deliver back the devil's name, but will say, "Va t'en."'[10]

The Parisian echo is surely superior to the Hibernian! Paddy Blake's simply understood and practised the common rules of good breeding; but the port Charenton echo is 'instinct with spirit,'[11] and endowed with a nice moral sense.

Amongst the famous bulls recorded by the illustrious Joe Miller,[12] there is one which has been continually quoted as an example of original Irish genius. An English gentleman was writing a letter in a coffee-house, and perceiving that an Irishman stationed behind him was taking that liberty which Hephæstion[13] used with his friend Alexander, instead of putting his seal upon the lips of the *curious impertinent*,[14] the English gentleman thought proper to reprove the Hibernian, if not with delicacy, at least with poetical justice: he concluded writing his letter in these words: 'I would say more, but a damned tall Irishman is reading over my shoulder every word I write.'

'You lie, you scoundrel!' said the self-convicted Hibernian.

This blunder is unquestionably excellent; but it is not originally Irish: it comes, with other riches, from the East, as the reader may find by looking into a book by M. Galland, entitled, 'The Remarkable Sayings of the Eastern Nations'.[15]

'A learned man was writing to a friend; a troublesome fellow was beside him, who was looking over his shoulder at what he was

---

* Natural History, century III. p. 191. – *Bacon produces it to show that echoes will not readily return the letter S.*

writing. The learned man, who perceived this, continued writing in these words, "If an impertinent chap, who stands beside me, were not looking at what I write, I would write many other things to you, which should be known only to you and to me."

'The troublesome fellow, who was reading on, now thought it incumbent upon him to speak, and said, "I swear to you, that I have not read or looked at what you are writing."

'The learned man replied, "Blockhead, as you are, why then do you say to me what you are now saying?"'*

Making allowance for the difference of manners in eastern and northern nations, there is, certainly, such a similarity between this oriental anecdote and Joe Miller's story, that we may conclude the latter is stolen from the former. Now, an *Irish* bull must be a species of blunder *peculiar* to Ireland; those that we have hitherto examined, though they may be called Irish Bulls by the ignorant vulgar, have no right, title, or claim to such a distinction. We should invariably exclude from that class all blunders which can be found in another country. For instance, a speech of the celebrated Irish beauty, lady C——, has been called a bull; but as a parallel can be produced in the speech of an English nobleman, *it tells for nothing*. When her ladyship was presented at court, his majesty, George the Second, politely hoped, 'that, since her arrival in England, she had been entertained with the gaieties of London.'

'O yes, please your majesty, I have seen every sight in London, worth seeing, except a coronation.'[16]

---

* 'Un savant écrivoit à un ami, et un importun étoit à côté de lui, qui regardoit par dessus l'épaule ce qu'il écrivoit. Le savant, qui s'en apperçut, écrivit ceci à la place: si un impertinent qui est à mon côté ne regardoit pas ce que j'écris, je vous écrirois encore plusieurs choses qui ne doivent être sues que de vous et de moi. L'importun, qui lisoit toujours, prit la parole et dit: "Je vous jure que je n'ai regardé ni lû ce que vous écrivois." Le savant repartit, "Ignorant, que vous êtes, pourquoi me dites-vous donc ce que vous dites?"' *Les Paroles remarquables des Orientaux; traduction de leurs ouvrages en Arabe, en Persan, et en Turc (suivant la copie imprimée à Paris), à la Haye, chez Louis et Henry Vandole, marchands libraires, dans le Pooten, à l'enseigne du Port Royal, M.DC.XCIV.*

This *naïveté* is certainly not equal to that of the English earl marshal, who, when his king found fault with some arrangement at his coronation, said, 'Please your majesty, I hope it will be better next time.'[17]

A *naïveté* of the same species entailed a heavy tax upon the inhabitants of Beaune, in France. Beaune is famous for burgundy; and Henry the Fourth, passing through his kingdom, stopped there, and was well entertained by his loyal subjects. His majesty praised the burgundy which they set before him – 'It was excellent! it was admirable!'

'O, sire!' cried they, 'do you think this excellent? *we have much finer* burgundy than this.'

'Have you so? then you can afford to pay for it,' replied Harry the Fourth; and he laid a double tax thenceforward upon the burgundy of Beaune.[18]

Of the same class of blunders is the following speech, which we actually heard not long ago from an Irishman:

'Please your worship, he sent me to the devil, and I came straight to your honour.'

We thought this an original Irish blunder, till we recollected its prototype in Marmontel's *Annette and Lubin*. Lubin concludes his harangue with, 'The bailiff sent us to the devil, and we come to put ourselves under your protection, my lord.'*

The French, at least in former times, were celebrated for politeness; yet we meet with a *naïve* compliment of a Frenchman, which would have been accounted a bull if it had been found in Ireland.

A gentleman was complimenting madame Denis on the manner in which she had just acted Zara.[19] 'To act that part,' said she, 'a person should be young and handsome.' 'Ah, madam!'

---

* 'Le bailli nous donne au diable, et nous nous recommandons à vous, monseigneur.'[20]

replied the complimenter *naïvement*, 'you are a complete proof of the contrary.'*

We know not any original Irish blunder superior to this, unless it be that which lord Orford pronounced to be the best bull that he ever heard.

'I hate that woman,' said a gentleman, looking at one who had been his nurse, 'I hate that woman, for she changed me at nurse.'[21]

Lord Orford particularly admires this bull, because in the confusion of the blunderer's ideas he is not clear even of his personal identity. Philosophers will not perhaps be so ready as his lordship has been to call this a blunder of the first magnitude. Those who have never been initiated into the mysteries of metaphysics may have the presumptuous ignorance to fancy that they understand what is meant by the common words *I*, or *me*; but the able metaphysician knows better than lord Orford's changeling how to prove, to our satisfaction, that we know nothing of the matter.

'Personal identity,' says Locke, 'consists not in the identity of substance, but in the identity of consciousness, wherein Socrates and the present mayor of Quinborough agree they are the same person: if the same Socrates, sleeping and waking, do not partake of the same consciousness, Socrates waking and sleeping is not the same person; and to punish Socrates waking for what sleeping Socrates thought, and waking Socrates was never conscious of, would be no more of right than to punish one twin for what his brother twin did, whereof he knew nothing, because their outsides are so like that they could not be distinguished; for such twins have been seen.'†

---

* On faisoit compliment à madame Denis de la façon, dont elle venoit de jouer Zaïre. 'Il faudroit,' dit elle, 'être belle et jeune.' 'Ah, madame!' reprit le complimenteur naïvement, vous êtes bien la preuve du contraire.'

† Locke's *Essay concerning the Human Understanding*, fifteenth edit. vol. i. p. 292.

We may presume that our Hibernian's consciousness could not retrograde to the time when he was changed at nurse; consequently there was no continuity of identity between the infant and the man who expressed his hatred of the nurse for perpetrating the fraud. At all events, the confusion of identity which excited lord Orford's admiration in our Hibernian is by no means unprecedented in France, England, or ancient Greece, and consequently it cannot be an instance of national idiosyncracy, or an Irish bull. We find a similar blunder in Spain, in the time of Cervantes:–

'Pray tell me, squire,' says the duchess, in *Don Quixote*, 'is not your master the person whose history is printed under the name of the sage Hidalgo Don Quixote de la Mancha, who professes himself the admirer of one Dulcinea del Toboso?'

'The very same, my lady,' answered Sancho; 'and I myself am that very squire of his, who is mentioned, or ought to be mentioned, in that history, *unless they have changed me in the cradle.*'[22]

In Molière's *Amphitrion* there is a dialogue between Mercure and Sosie evidently taken from the *attic* Lucian.[23] Sosie being completely puzzled out of his personal identity, if not out of his senses, says literally, 'of my being myself I begin to doubt in good earnest; yet when I feel myself, and when I recollect myself, it seems to me that *I am I.*'*

We see that the puzzle about identity proves at last to be of Grecian origin. It is really edifying to observe how those things which have long been objects of popular admiration shrink and fade when exposed to the light of strict examination. An experienced critic proposed that a work should be written to inquire into the pretensions of modern writers to original invention, to trace their thefts, and to restore the property to the ancient owners. Such

---

* De moi je commence à douter tout de bon.
   Pourtant quand je me tâte, et quand je me rapelle,
   Il me semble que je suis moi.'[24]

a work would require powers and erudition beyond what can be expected from any ordinary individual; the labour must be shared amongst numbers, and we are proud to assist in ascertaining the rightful property even of bulls and blunders; though without pretending, like some literary blood-hounds, to follow up a plagiarism, where common sagacity is at a fault.

Chapter II

Irish Newspapers

We presume that we have successfully disputed the claims imposed upon the public, in behalf of certain spurious, alien blunders, pretending to be native, original Irish bulls; and we shall now with pleasure proceed to examine those which have better titles to notice. Even nonsense ceases to be worthy of attention and public favour, unless it be original.

'Dear lady Emily,' says Miss Allscrip, in the excellent comedy of the Heiress – 'Dear lady Emily, don't you dote upon folly?'

'To ecstacy!' replies her ladyship; 'I only despair of seeing it well kept up.'[25]

We flatter ourselves 'there is no great danger of that,' for we have the Irish newspapers before us, where, no doubt, we shall find a fresh harvest of indigenous absurdity ripe for the sickle.

The first advertisement that meets our eye is promising.

It is the late proclamation of an Irish mayor, in which we are informed, that certain business is to be transacted in that city 'every Monday (Easter Sunday only excepted).' This seems rather an unnecessary exception; but it is not an inadvertency, caused by any hurry of business in his worship; it is deliberately copied from a precedent, set in England, by a baronet formerly well known in parliament, who, in the preamble to a bill, proposed that certain regulations should take place 'on every Monday (Tuesday excepted).'[26] We fear, also, that an English mayor has been known to blunder. Some years ago the mayor of a capital English city published a proclamation and advertisement, previous to the races, 'that no gentleman will be allowed to ride on the course, but *the horses* that are to run.'[27] A mayor's blundering proclamation is not, however, worth half so much in the eye of ridicule as a lord lieutenant's.

'A saint in crape is twice a saint in lawn.'[28]

A bull on the throne is worth twice as much as a bull in the chair.

'By the lord lieutenant and council[29] of Ireland.
'A proclamation.
****,

'Whereas the greatest economy is necessary in the consumption of *all species of grain, and, especially, in the consumption of potatoes*, &c.
'Given at the council chamber in Dublin.'

This is the first time we have been informed, by authority, that potatoes are a species of grain; but we must accede to this new botanical arrangement, when published under such splendid auspices. The assertion, certainly, is not made in distinct terms; but all who understand the construction of language must imply the conclusion that we draw from these premises. A general position is in the first member of the sentence laid down, '*that the greatest economy is necessary in the consumption of all species of grain.*' A particular exemplification of the principle is made in the next clause, '*especially in the consumption of potatoes.*'

The inference is as plain as can be made.

The next article in our newspaper is an advertisement of lands to be let to *an improving tenant*: – 'A few miles from Cork, in *a most sporting country*, bounded by an *uncommon fine* turf bog, on the verge of which there are a number of fine *lime kilns*, where *that manure* may be had on very moderate terms, the distance for carriage not being many hundred yards. The whole lands being now in great heart, and completely laid down, entirely surrounded and divided by *inpenetrable furze ditches, made of quarried stone laid edgeways.*'[30]

It will be a matter of difficulty to the untravelled English reader to comprehend how furze ditches can be made of quarried stones laid edgeways, or any way; and we fear that we should only puzzle his intellects still more if we should attempt to explain to him the mysteries of Irish ditching in the technical terms of the country. With the face of a ditch he may be acquainted, but to *the back* and *gripe*, and bottom of the gripe, and top of the back of a ditch, we fear he is still to be introduced.

We can never sufficiently admire these furze ditches made of quarried stones; they can, indeed, be found only in Ireland: but we have heard in England of things almost as extraordinary. Dr Grey, in his erudite and entertaining notes on Hudibras, records the disposition of a lawyer, who, in an action of battery, told the judge 'that the defendant beat his client with a certain *wooden instrument* called *an iron pestle.*'[31] Nay, to go further still, a wise annotator on the Pentateuch, named Peter Harrison, observed of Moses's two *tables of stone*, that they were made of *shittim-wood*.[32] The stone furze ditches are scarcely bolder instances of the catachresis than the stone tables of shittim-wood. This bold figure of rhetoric in an Irish advertisement of an estate may lead us to expect that Hibernian advertisers may, in time, emulate the fame of Christie,[33] the prince of auctioneers, whose fine descriptive powers can make more of an estate on paper than ever was made of it in any other shape, except in the form of an ejectment. The fictions of law, indeed, surpass even the auctioneer's imagination; and a man may be said never to know the extent of his own possessions until he is served with a process of ejectment. He then finds himself required to give up the possession of a multitude of barns, orchards, fish-ponds, horse-ponds, dwelling-houses, pigeon-houses, dove-cotes, out-houses, and appurtenances, which he never saw or heard of, and which are nowhere to be found upon the surface of the habitual globe; so that we cannot really express this English legal transaction without being guilty of an Irish bull, and saying that the person ejected is *ousted* from places which he never entered.

To proceed with our newspapers. – The next advertisement is from a schoolmaster: but we shall not descant upon its grammatical errors, because they are not blunders peculiar to Irish schoolmasters. We have frequently observed that the advertisements of schoolmasters, even in England, are seldom free from solecisms: too much care in writing, it seems, is almost as bad as too little. In the preface of the dictionary of the French Academy,[34] there are, as it is computed by an able French critic, no less than sixteen faults; and in Harris, the celebrated grammarian's dedication of his *Hermes*,[35] there is one bull, and almost as many faults as lines. It appears as if the most precise and learned writers sometimes, like the ladies in one of Congreve's plays, 'run into the danger to avoid the apprehension.'[36]

After a careful scrutiny of the Hibernian advertisements, we are compelled to confess that we have not met with any blunders that more nearly resemble our notion of an Irish bull than one which, some years ago, appeared in our English papers. It was the title to an advertisement of a washing machine, in these words: 'Every *man* his own *Washerwoman*!' We have this day, Nov. 19, 1807, seen the following: 'This day were published, Memoirs of the Life of Mrs Elizabeth Carter,[37] with a *new edition* of her Poems, some of which have *never* before appeared.' And an eye-witness assures us, that lately he saw an advertisement in the following terms, stuck up on the walls of an English coffee-house: 'This coffee-house removed up stairs!'

A Roman emperor used to draw his stairs up after him every night into his bedchamber,[38] and we have heard of throwing a house out of the windows; but drawing a whole house up into itself is new.

How can we account for such a blunder, in an advertisement on the wall of an English coffee-house, except by supposing that it was penned by an Irish waiter? If that were the case, it would be an admirable example of an Irish bull! and therefore we had best take it for granted.

Let not any conscientious person be startled at the mode of reasoning by which we have convicted an imaginary Irish waiter of a real bull: it is at least as good, if not better logic, than that which was successfully employed in the time of the *popish plot*, to convict an Irish physician of forgery. The matter is thus recorded by L'Estrange. The Irish physician 'was charged with writing a treasonable libel, but denied the thing, and appealed to the unlikeness of the characters. It was agreed that there was no resemblance at all in the hands; but asserted that the doctor had two hands; his *physic hand* and his *plot hand*, and the one not a jot like the other. Now this was the doctor's plot hand, and it was insisted that, because it was not like one of his hands, it must be like the other.'[39]

By this convenient mode of reasoning, an Irishman may, at any time, be convicted of any crime, or of any absurdity.

But what have we next in our newspaper? – 'Murder, Robbery, and Reward.' This seems a strange connexion of things, according to our vulgar notions of distributive justice; but we are told that the wicked shall have their *reward* even in this world; and we suppose it is upon this principle, that over the stocks in a town in Ireland there appears this inscription: 'A reward for vagabonds.'

Upon proceeding further in our advertisement, which begins with 'Murder, Robbery, and Reward,' we find, however, that contrary to the just expectations raised by the title, the reward is promised, not to the robbers and murderers, but to those who shall discover and prosecute them to conviction. Here we were led into error by that hasty mode of elision which sometimes obtains in the titles even of our English law processes; as sci-fa, fi-fa, qui-tam, &c.; names which, to preserve the glorious uncertainty of the law, never refer to the sense, but to the first words of the writs.[40]

In our newspaper, a formidable list of unanimous resolutions of various committees and corps succeeds to the advertisement of murder, robbery, and reward; and we have, at the close of each day's business, thanksgivings, in various formulas, for the very proper, upright, or spirited behaviour of our worthy, gallant, or respected chairman. Now that a man may behave properly, or sit uprightly in a chair, we can readily comprehend; but what are we to understand by a *spirited* behaviour in a chair? Perhaps it alludes to the famous duel fought by a gouty Irish gentleman in his arm chair. As the gallant chairman actually in that position shot his adversary, it behoves us to *understand* the meaning of spirited behaviour in the chair.[41]

We may, however, venture to hint, fas est et ab hoste doceri,[42] that in the publications of corps and committees, this formula should be omitted – 'Resolved *unanimously* (with only *one* dissentient voice.)' Here the obloquy, meant to rest on the one dissentient voice, unfortunately falls upon the publishers of the disgrace, exposing them to the ridicule of resolving an Irish bull. If this be a bull, however, we are concerned to find it is matched by that of the government of Munich, who published a catalogue of forbidden books, and afterwards, under heavy penalties, forbade the reading of the catalogue.[43] But this might be done in the hurry occasioned by the just dread of revolutionary principles.

What shall we say for the blunder of a French academician, in a time of profound peace, who gave it as his opinion, that nothing should be read in the public sittings of the academy 'par dela ce qui est imposé par les statuts: il motivait son avis en disant – En fait d'*inutilités* il ne faut que *le necessaire.*'[44] If this speech had been made by a member of the Royal Irish Academy,[45] it would have had the honour to be noticed all over England as a bull. *The honour to be noticed*, we say, in imitation of the exquisitely polite expression of a correspondent of the English Royal Society,[46] who talks of 'the earthquake that had the honour to be noticed by the Royal Society.'

It will, we fear, be long before the Irish emerge so far from barbarism as to write in this style. The Irish are, however, we are happy to observe, making some little approaches to a refined and courtly style; kings, and in imitation of them, great men, and all who think themselves great – a numerous class – speak and write as much as possible in the plural number instead of the singular. Instead of *I*, they always say *we*; instead of *my*, *our*, according to the Italian idiom, which flatters this humour so far as to make it a point of indispensable politeness. It is, doubtless, in humble imitation of such illustrious examples, that an Irishman of the lowest class, when he means to express that he is a member of a committee, says, *I am a committee.* Thus consolidating the power, wisdom, and virtue of a whole committee in his own person. Superior even to the Indian, who believes that he shall inherit the powers and virtues of his enemies after he has destroyed them;* this committee-man takes

---

* 'So Indian murd'rers hope to gain
The powers and virtues of the slain,
Of wretches they destroy.'[47]

possession of the faculties of his living friends and associates. When some of the *united men*, as they call themselves, were examined, they frequently answered to the questions, who, or what are you? I am a com´mittē ē.[48]

However extraordinary it may at first sound, to hear one man assert that he is a whole committee, it is not more wonderful than that the whole parliament of Bordeaux should be found in a one-horse chair.*

We forbear to descant farther upon Irish committee-men, lest we should call to mind, merely by the similarity of name, the times when England had her committee-men, who were not perfectly free from all tinge of absurdity. It is remarkable, that in times of popular ferment, a variety of new terms are coined to serve purposes and passions of the moment. In the days of the English committee-men this practice had risen to such a height, that it was fair game for ridicule. Accordingly, sir John Birkenhead, about that time, found it necessary to publish '*The Children's Dictionary; an exact Collection of all New Words born since Nov. 3, 1640, in Speeches, Prayers, and Sermons, as well those that signify something as nothing.*'[49] We observe that it has been likewise found necessary to publish, in France, *une Dictionnaire néologique*,[50] a dictionary of the new terms adopted since the revolution.

It must be supposed, that during the late disturbances in Ireland,[51] many *cant* terms have been brought into use, which are not yet to be reckoned amongst the acknowledged terms of the country. However absurd these may be, they are not for our purpose proper subjects of animadversion. Some countries have their birds of passage, and some their follies of passage, which it is scarcely worth while to shoot as they fly. It has often been said, that the language of a people is a just criterion of their progress in

---

* Vide Mémoires du Cardinal de Retz.[52]

civilization; but we must not take a specimen of their vocabulary during the immediate prevalence of any transient passion or prejudice. It is to be hoped, that all party barbarisms in language will now be disused and forgotten; for some time has elapsed since we read the following article of country intelligence in a Dublin paper: —

'General —— scoured the country yesterday, but had not the good fortune to meet with a single rebel.'[53]

The author of this paragraph seems to have been a keen sportsman; he regrets the not meeting with a single rebel, as he would the not meeting with a single hare or partridge; and he justly considers the human biped as fair game, to be hunted down by all who are properly qualified and licensed by government. To the English, perhaps, it may seem a strange subject of lamentation, that a general could not meet with a single rebel in the county of Wicklow, when they have so lately been informed from the high authority of a noble lord, that Ireland was so disturbed, that whenever he went out, he called as regularly for his pistols as for his hat and gloves.[54] Possibly, however, this was only a figure of speech, like that of bishop Wilkins, who prophesied that the time would come when gentlemen, when they were to go a journey, would call for their wings as regularly as they call for their boots.[55] – We *believe* that the hyperboles of the privy-counsellor and the bishop are of equal magnitude.

Chapter III

The Criminal Law of Bulls and Blunders

Madame de Sevigné observes, that there are few people sufficiently candid, or sufficiently enlightened, to distinguish, in their judgments of others, between those faults and mistakes which proceed from *manque d'esprit*, and those which arise merely from *manque d'usage*.[56] We cannot appreciate the talents or character of foreigners, without making allowance for their ignorance of our manners, of the idiom of our language, and the multifarious significations of some of our words. A French gentleman, who dined in London, in company with the celebrated author of the Rambler, wishing to show him a mark of peculiar respect, drank Dr Johnson's health in these words: 'Your health, Mr Vagabond.'[57] Assuredly no well-judging Englishman would undervalue the Frenchman's abilities, because he mistook the meaning of the words Vagabond and Rambler; he would recollect, that in old English and modern French authors, vagabond means wanderer: des eaux vagabondes is a phrase far from inelegant. But independently of this consideration, no well-bred gentleman would put a foreigner out of countenance by openly laughing at such a mistake: he would imitate the politeness of the Frenchman, who, when Dr Moore said, 'I am afraid the expression I have just used is not French,' replied, 'Non, monsieur – mais il mérite bien de l'être.'[58] It would, indeed, be a great stretch of politeness to extend this to our Irish neighbours: for no Irishism can ever deserve to be Anglicised, though so many Gallicisms have of late not only been naturalised in England, but even adopted by the most fashionable speakers and writers. The mistaking a feminine for a masculine noun, or a masculine for a feminine, must, in all probability, have happened to every Englishman that ever opened his lips in Paris; yet without losing his reputation for common sense. But when a poor Irish haymaker, who had but just learned a few phrases of the English language by rote, mistook a feminine for a masculine noun, and began his speech in a court of justice with these words: 'My lord, I am a poor widow,' instead of 'My lord, I am a poor widower;' it was sufficient to throw a grave judge and jury into convulsions of laughter. It was formerly, in law, no murder to kill a *merus Hibernicus*;[59] and it is to this day no offence against good manners to laugh at any of this species. It is of a thousand times more consequence to have the laugh than the argument on our side, as all those know full well who have any experience in the management of the great or little vulgar. By the common custom and courtesy of England we *have* the laugh on our side: let us keep it by all means. All means are justifiable to obtain a great end, as all great men maintain in practice, if not in theory. We need not, in imitating them, have any scruples of conscience; we need not apprehend, that to ridicule our Hibernian neighbours unmercifully is unfriendly or ungenerous. Nations, it has been well observed, are never generous in their conduct towards each other. We must follow the common *custom* of nations where we have no *law* to guide our proceedings. We must therefore carefully continue the laudable practice of ridiculing the blunders, whether real or imaginary, of Irishmen. In conversation, Englishmen are permitted sometimes to blunder, but without ever being called blunderers. It would, indeed, be an intolerable restraint upon social intercourse, if every man were subject to be taxed for each inaccuracy of language – if he were compelled to talk, upon all occasions, as if he were amenable to a star-chamber of criticism, and surrounded by informers.[60]

Much must be allowed in England for the licence of conversation; but by no means must this conversation-licence be extended to the Irish. If, for instance, at the convivial hour of dinner, when men are not usually intent upon grammatical or mathematical niceties, an Irish gentleman desires him 'who rules his roast,' to cut the sirloin of beef *horizontally downwards*, let the mistake immediately be set down in our note-books, and conned over and got by heart; and let it be repeated to all eternity as a bull. But if an English lady observe, when the candles have long stood unsnuffed, that 'those odious long wicks will soon grow up to the ceiling,' she can be accused only of an error of vision. We conjure our readers to attend to these distinctions in their intercourse with their Hibernian neighbours: it must be done habitually and technically; and we must not listen to what is called reason; we must not enter into any argument, pro or con, but silence every Irish opponent, if we can, with a laugh.

The abbé Girard, in his accurate work, 'Synonymes François,'[61] makes a *plausible* distinction between *une âne* et *un ignorant*; he says, 'On est âne par disposition: on est ignorant par defaut d'instruction.' An ignorant person may certainly, even in the very circumstances which betray his ignorance, evince considerable ability. For instance, the native Indian, who for the first time saw a bottle of porter uncorked, and who expressed great astonishment at the quantity of froth which he saw burst from the bottle, and much curiosity to know whether it could all be put in again, showed even in his ignorance a degree of capacity, which in different situations might have saved his life, or have made his fortune. In the situation of the poor fisherman, and the great giant of smoke, who issued from the small vessel, well known to all versed in the Arabian Tales,[62] such acuteness would have saved his life; and a similar spirit of inquiry, applied to chemistry, might, in modern times, have made his fortune. Even where no positive abilities are displayed at the time by those who manifest ignorance, we should not (*except the culprits be natives of Ireland*) hastily give them up. Ignorance of the most common objects is not only incident to certain situations, but absolutely unavoidable; and the individuals placed in those situations are no more blameable than they would be for becoming blind in the snows of Lapland, or for having goitres amongst the Cretins of le Vallais.[63] Would you blame the ignorant nuns, who, insensible of the danger of an eruption of Mount Vesuvius,* warmed themselves at the burning lava which flowed up to the windows of their cells? or would you think the French canoness an idiot, who, at the age of fifty, was, on account of her health, to go out of her convent, and asked, when she met a cow for the first time, what strange animal that was? or would you think that those poor children deserved to be stigmatised as fools, who, after being confined for a couple of years in an English workhouse, actually at eight years old had forgotten the names of a pig and a calf:† their ignorance was surely more deplorable than ridiculous. When the London young lady kept a collection of chicken-bones on her plate at dinner, as a bonne-bouche for her brother's horse,‡ Dr Johnson would not suffer her to be called an idiot, but very judiciously defended her, by maintaining, that her action merely demonstrated her ignorant of points of natural history, on which a London miss had no immediate opportunity of obtaining information. Had the world always judged upon such subjects with similar candour, the reproachful cant term of *cockney* would never have been disgracefully naturalised in the English language. This word, as we are informed by a learned philologist, originated from the mistake of a learned citizen's son, who having been bred up entirely in the metropolis, was so gloriously ignorant of country life and country animals, that the first time he heard a *cock* crow, he called it *neighing*.[64] If such a mistake had been made by an Irishman, it would surely have been called a bull: it has, at least, as good pretensions to the

---

* Vide Sir W. Hamilton's account of an eruption of Mount Vesuvius.[65]

† This fact, *we believe*, is mentioned in a letter of Mrs Cappe's on parish schools.[66]

‡ Vide Mrs Piozzi's *English Synonymy*.[67]

title as many mistakes made by ignorant Hibernians; for instance, the well-known blunder relative to the sphinx: – An uninformed Irishman, hearing the sphinx alluded to in company, whispered to a friend, 'The sphinx! who is that now?'

'A monster man.'

'Oh, a *Munster*-man: I thought he was from Connaught,'[68] replied our Irishman, determined not to seem totally unacquainted with the family. Gross and ridiculous as this blunder appears, we are compelled by candour to allow, that the affectation of showing knowledge has betrayed to shame men far superior to our Hibernian, both in reputation and in the means of acquiring knowledge.

Cardinal Richelieu, the Mecænas or would-be Mecænas of France, once mistook the name of a noted grammarian, *Maurus Terentianus*, for a play of Terence's. This is called by the French writer who records it, 'une *bévue* bien grossière.'[69] However gross, a mistake can never be made into a bull. We find *bévues* French, English, Italian, German, Latin, and Greek, of theologians, historians, antiquarians, poets, critics, and translators, without end. The learned Budæus takes sir Thomas More's Utopia for a true history;[70] and proposes sending missionaries to work in the conversion of so wise a people as the Utopians. An English antiquarian* mistakes a tomb in a Gothic cathedral for the tomb of Hector. Pope, our great poet, and prince of translators, mistakes *Dec. the 8th*, *Nov. the 5th*, of Cinthio, for Dec. 8th, Nov. 5th; and Warburton, his learned critic, improves upon the blunder, by afterward writing the words December and November at full length.[71] Better still, because more comic, is the blunder of a Frenchman, who, puzzled by the title of one of Cibber's plays, 'Love's Last Shift,'[72] translates it 'La Dernière Chemise de l'Amour.' We laugh at these mistakes, and forget them; but who can forget the blunder of the Cork almanac-maker, who

---

* John Lydgate.[73]

informs the world that the principal republics in *Europe* are Venice, Holland, and *America*?

The blunders of men of all countries, except Ireland, do not affix an indelible stigma upon individual or national character. A free pardon is, and ought to be, granted by every Englishman to the vernacular and literary errors of those who have the happiness to be born subjects of Great Britain. What enviable privileges are annexed to the birth of an Englishman! and what a misfortune it is to be a native of Ireland!

Chapter IV

Little Dominick

We have laid down the general law of bulls and blunders; but as there is no rule without an exception, we may perhaps allow an exception in favour of little Dominick.

Little Dominick was born at Fort-Reilly,[74] in Ireland, and bred nowhere until his tenth year, when he was sent to Wales to learn manners and grammar at the school of Mr Owen ap Davies ap Jenkins ap Jones. This gentleman had reason to think himself the greatest of men; for he had over his chimney-piece a well-smoked genealogy, duly attested, tracing his ancestry in a direct line up to Noah; and moreover he was nearly related to the learned etymologist, who, in the time of Queen Elizabeth wrote a folio to prove that the language of Adam and Eve in Paradise was pure Welsh.[75] With such causes to be proud, Mr Owen ap Davies ap Jenkins ap Jones was excusable for sometimes seeming to forget that a schoolmaster is but a man. He, however, sometimes entirely forgot that a boy is but a boy; and this happened most frequently with respect to little Dominick.

This unlucky wight[76] was flogged every morning by his master, not for his vices, but for his vicious constructions, and laughed at by his companions every evening for his idiomatic absurdities. They would probably have been inclined to sympathise in his misfortunes, but that he was the only Irish boy at school; and as he was at a distance from all his relations, and without a friend to take his part, he was a just object of obloquy and derision. Every sentence he spoke was a bull; every two words he put together proved a false concord; and every sound he articulated betrayed the brogue.[77] But as he possessed some of the characteristic boldness of those who have been dipped in the Shannon, he showed himself able and willing to fight his own battles with the host of foes by whom he was encompassed. Some of these, it was said, were of nearly twice his stature. This may be exaggerated, but it is certain that our hero sometimes ventured with sly Irish humour to revenge himself upon his most powerful tyrant by mimicking the Welsh accent, in which Mr Owen ap Jones said to him, 'Cot pless me, you plockit, and shall I never *learn* you Enclish crammer?'[78]

It was whispered in the ear of this Dionysius, that our little hero was a mimic; and he was treated with increased severity.

The midsummer holydays approached; but he feared that they would shine no holydays for him. He had written to his mother to tell her that school would break up the 21st, and to beg an answer, without fail, by return of post; but no answer came.

It was now nearly two months since he had heard from his dear mother or any of his friends in Ireland. His spirits began to sink under the pressure of these accumulated misfortunes: he slept little, ate less, and played not at all; indeed nobody would play with him upon equal terms, because he was nobody's equal; his schoolfellows continued to consider him as a being, if not of a different species, at least of a different *caste* from themselves.

Mr Owen ap Jones's triumph over the little Irish plockit was nearly complete, for the boy's heart was almost broken, when there came to the school a new scholar – O, how unlike the others! His name was Edwards; he was the son of a neighbouring Welsh gentleman; and he had himself the spirit of a gentleman. When he saw how poor Dominick was persecuted, he took him under his protection, fought his battles with the Welsh boys, and, instead of laughing at him for speaking Irish, he endeavoured to teach him to speak English. In his answers to the first question Edwards ever asked him, little Dominick made two blunders, which set all his other companions in a roar; yet Edwards would not allow them to be genuine bulls.

In answer to the question, 'Who is your father?' Dominick said, with a deep sigh, 'I have no father – I am an orphan* – I have only a mother.'

'Have you any brothers and sisters?'

'No; I wish I had; perhaps they would love me, and not laugh at me,' said Dominick, with tears in his eyes; 'but I have no brothers but myself.'

One day Mr Jones came into the school-room with an open letter in his hand, saying, 'Here, you little Irish plockit, here's a letter from your mother.'

The little Irish blockhead started from his form, and, throwing his grammar on the floor, leaped up higher than he or any boy in the school had ever been seen to leap before, and, clapping his

---

* Iliad, 6th book, l. 432, Andromache says to Hector, 'You will make your son an orphan, and your wife a widow.'

hands, he exclaimed, 'A letter from my mother! And *will* I hear the letter? And *will* I see her once more? And *will* I go home these holydays? O, then I will be too happy!'

'There's no tanger of that,' said Mr Owen ap Jones; 'for your mother, like a wise ooman, writes me here, that py the atvice of your cardian, to oom she is coing to be married, she will not pring you home to Ireland till I send her word you are perfect in your Enclish crammer at least.'

'I have my lesson perfect, sir,' said Dominick, taking his grammar up from the floor, '*will* I say it now?'

'*Will* I say it now? No, you plockit, no, and I will write your mother word you have proke Priscian's head[79] four times this tay, since her letter came. You Irish plockit!' continued the relentless grammarian, 'will you never learn the tifference between *shall* and *will*? *Will* I hear the letter, and *will* I see her once more? What Enclish is this, plockit?'

The Welsh boys all grinned, except Edwards, who hummed, loud enough to be heard, two lines of the good old English song,

> 'And *will* I see him once again?
> And *will* I hear him speak?'[80]

Many of the boys were fortunately too ignorant to feel the force of the quotation; but Mr Owen ap Jones understood it, turned upon his heel, and walked off. Soon afterwards he summoned Dominick to his awful desk; and, pointing with his ruler to the following page in Harris's *Hermes*[81] bade him 'reat it, and unterstant it, if he could.' Little Dominick read, but could not understand.

'Then reat it loud, you plockit.'

Dominick read aloud –

'There is *nothing appears so clearly* an object of the mind or intellect only as *the future* does, since we can find no place for its existence any where else: not but the same, if we consider, is *equally true* of the past –.'

'Well, co on – What stops the plockit? Can't you reat Enclish now?'

'Yes, sir; but I was trying to understand it. I was considering, that this is like what they would call an Irish bull, if I had said it.'

Little Dominick could not explain what he meant in English, that Mr Owens ap Jones *would* understand; and, to punish him for his impertinent observation, the boy was doomed to learn all that Harris and Lowth[82] have written to explain the nature of *shall* and *will.* The reader, if he be desirous of knowing the full extent of the penance enjoined, may consult Lowth's *Grammar*, p. 52, ed. 1799, and Harris's *Hermes*, p. 10, 11, and 12, 4th edition. Undismayed at the length of this task, little Dominick only said, 'I hope, if I say it all without missing a word, you will not give my mother a bad account of me and my grammar studies, sir.'

'Say it all first, without missing a word, and then I shall see what I shall say,' replied Mr Owen ap Jones.

Even the encouragement of this oracular answer excited the boy's fond hopes so keenly, that he lent his little soul to the task, learned it perfectly, said it at night, without missing one word, to his friend Edwards, and said it the next morning, without missing one word, to his master.

'And now, sir,' said the boy, looking up, 'will you write to my mother? And *shall* I see her? And *shall* I go home?'

'Tell me first, whether you understant all this that you have learnt so cliply,'[83] said Mr Owen ap Jones.

That was more than his bond. Our hero's countenance fell: and he acknowledged that he did not understand it perfectly.

'Then I cannot write a coot account of you and your crammer studies to your mother; my conscience coes against it,' said the conscientious Mr Owen ap Jones.

No entreaties could move him. Dominick never saw the letter that was written to his mother; but he felt the consequence. She wrote word this time punctually *by return of the post*, that she was sorry that she could not send for him home these holydays, as she heard so bad an account from Mr Jones, &c. and as she thought it her duty not to interrupt the course of his education, especially his grammar studies. Little Dominick heaved many a sigh when he saw the packings up of all his school-fellows, and dropped a few tears as he looked out of the window, and saw them, one after another, get on their Welsh ponies, and gallop off towards their homes.

'I have no home to go to,' said he.

'Yes, you have,' cried Edwards; 'and *our* horses are at the door to carry us there.'

'To Ireland? me! the horses!' said the poor boy, quite bewildered: 'and will they bring me to Ireland?'

'No; the horses cannot carry you to Ireland,' said Edwards, laughing good-naturedly, 'but you have a home now in England. I asked my father to let me *take* you home with me; and he says "Yes," like a dear good father, and has sent the horses. Come let's away.'

'But will Mr Jones let me go?'

'Yes; he dare not refuse; for my father has a living in his gift that Jones wants, and which he will not have, if he do not change his tune to you.'

Little Dominick could not speak one word, his heart was so full. No boy could be happier than he was during these holydays: 'the genial current of his soul,'[84] which had been frozen by unkindness, flowed with all its natural freedom and force.

When Dominick returned to school after these holydays were over, Mr Owen ap Jones, who now found that the Irish boy had an English protector with a living in his gift, changed his tone. He never more complained unjustly that Dominick broke Priscian's head, seldom called him Irish plockit, and once would have flogged a Welsh boy for taking up this cast-off expression of the master's, but the Irish blockhead begged the culprit off.

Little Dominick sprang forward rapidly in his studies: he soon surpassed every boy in the school, his friend Edwards only excepted. In process of time, his guardian removed him to a higher seminary of education. Edwards had a tutor at home. The friends separated. Afterwards they followed different professions in distant parts of the world; and they neither saw nor heard any more of each other for many years. From boys they grew into men, and Dominick, now no longer little Dominick, went over to India as private secretary to one of our commanders in chief. How he got into this situation, or by what gradations he rose in the world, we are not exactly informed: we know only that he was the reputed author of a much-admired pamphlet on Indian affairs, that the despatches of the general to whom he was secretary were remarkably well written, and that Dominick O'Reilly, esq. returned to England, after several years' absence, not miraculously rich, but with a fortune equal to his wishes. His wishes were not extravagant: his utmost ambition was to return to his native country with a fortune that should enable him to live independently of all the world, especially of some of his relations, who had not used him well. His mother was no more.

Upon his arrival in London, one of the first things he did was to read the Irish newspapers. – To his inexpressible joy, he saw the estate of Fort-Reilly advertised to be sold – the very estate which had formerly belonged to his own family. Away he posted directly to an attorney's, who was empowered to dispose of the land.

When this attorney produced a map of the well-known pleasure-ground, and an elevation of that house in which he had spent the happiest hours of his infancy, his heart was so touched, that he was on the point of paying down more for an old ruin than a good new house would cost. The attorney acted *honestly by his client*, and seized this moment to exhibit a plan of the stabling and offices,

Little Dominick

which, as sometimes is the case in Ireland, were in a style far superior to the dwelling-house. Our hero surveyed these with transport. He rapidly planned various improvements in imagination, and planted certain favourite spots in the pleasure-ground. During this time the attorney was giving directions to a clerk about some other business: suddenly the name of *Owen ap Jones* struck his ear – He started.

'Let him wait in the front parlour: his money is not forthcoming,' said the attorney; 'and if he keeps Edwards in gaol till he rots —'

'Edwards! Good heavens! – in gaol! What Edwards?' exclaimed our hero.

It was his friend Edwards.

The attorney told him that Mr Edwards had been involved in great distress by taking upon himself his father's debts, which had been incurred in exploring a mine in Wales; that of all the creditors none had refused to compound, except a Welsh parson, who had been presented to his living by old Edwards; and that this Mr Owen ap Jones had thrown young Mr Edwards into gaol for the debt.

'What is the rascal's demand? He shall be paid off this instant,' cried Dominick, throwing down the plan of Fort-Reilly: 'send for him up, and let me pay him off upon the spot.'

'Had not we best finish our business first, about the O'Reilly estate, sir?' said the attorney.

'No, sir; damn the O'Reilly estate,' cried he, huddling the maps together on the desk, and taking up the bank notes, which he had begun to reckon for the purchase money. 'I beg your pardon, sir. If you knew the facts, you would excuse me. Why does not this rascal come up to be paid?'

The attorney, thunderstruck by this Hibernian impetuosity, had not yet found time to take his pen out of his mouth. As he sat transfixed in his armchair, O'Reilly ran to the head of the stairs, and called out in a stentorian voice, 'Here, you Mr Owen ap Jones'; come up and be paid off this instant, or you shall never be paid *at all.*'

Up stairs hobbled the old schoolmaster, as fast as the gout and Welsh ale would let him. 'Cot pless me, that voice,' he began –

'Where's your bond, sir?' said the attorney.

'Safe here, Cot be praised,' said the terrified Owen ap Jones, pulling out of his bosom, first a blue pocket-handkerchief, and then a tattered Welsh grammar, which O'Reilly kicked to the farther end of the room.

'Here is my pond,' said he, 'in the crammer,' which he gathered from the ground; then fumbling over the leaves, he at length unfolded the precious deposit.

O'Reilly saw the bond, seized it, looked at the sum, paid it into the attorney's hands, tore the seal from the bond; then, without looking at old Jones, whom he dared not trust himself to speak to, he clapped his hat upon his head, and rushed out of the room. Arrived at the King's Bench prison, he hurried to the apartment where Edwards was confined. The bolts flew back; for even the turnkeys seemed to catch our hero's enthusiasm.

'Edwards, my dear boy! how do you do? Here's a bond debt, justly due to you for my education. O, never mind asking any unnecessary questions; only just make haste out of this undeserved abode: our old rascal is paid off – Owen ap Jones, you know. – Well, how the man stares! Why, now, will you have the assurance to pretend to forget who I am? and must I *spake*,' continued he, assuming the tone of his childhood, 'and must I *spake* to you again in my ould Irish brogue, before you will ricollict your own *little Dominick*?'

When his friend Edwards was out of prison, and when our hero had leisure to look into business, he returned to the attorney, to see that Mr Owen ap Jones had been legally satisfied.

'Sir,' said the attorney, 'I have paid the plaintiff in this suit; and he is satisfied: but I must say,' added he, with a contemptuous smile, 'that you Irish gentlemen are rather in too great a hurry in doing business: business, sir, is a thing that must be done slowly to be done well.'

'I am ready now to do business as slowly as you please; but when my friend was in prison, I thought the quicker I did the business the better. Now tell me what mistake I have made, and I will rectify it instantly.'

'*Instantly!* 'Tis well, sir, with your promptitude, that you have to deal with what prejudice thinks uncommon – an honest attorney. Here are some bank notes of yours, sir, amounting to a good round sum. You made a little blunder in this business: you left me the penalty, instead of the principal, of the bond – just twice as much as you should have done.'

'Just twice as much as was in the bond, but not twice as much as I should have done, nor half as much as I should have done, in my opinion,' said O'Reilly; 'but whatever I did was with my eyes open: I was persuaded you were an honest man; in which you see I was not mistaken; and as a man of business, I knew you would pay Jones only his due. The remainder of the money I meant, and mean, should lie in your hands for my friend Edwards's use. I feared he would not have taken it from my hands: I therefore left it in yours. To have taken my friend out of prison merely to let him go back again to-day, for want of money to keep himself clear with the world, would have been a blunder indeed, but not an Irish blunder: our Irish blunders are never blunders of the heart.'

Chapter V

The Bliss of Ignorance

No *well-informed* Englishman would laugh at the blunders of such a character as little Dominick; but there are people who justify the assertion, that laughter always rises from a sense of real or imaginary superiority. Now if it be true, that laughter has its source of vanity, as the most ignorant are generally the most vain, they must enjoy this pleasure in its highest perfection. Unconscious of their own deficiencies, and consequently fearless of becoming in their turn the objects of ridicule, they enjoy in full security the delight of humbling their superiors. How much are they to be admired for the courage with which they apply, on all occasions, their test of truth! Wise men may be struck with admiration, respect, doubt, or humility; but the ignorant, happily unconscious that they know nothing, can be checked in their merriment by no consideration, human or divine. Theirs is the sly sneer, the dry joke, and the horse laugh: theirs the comprehensive range of ridicule, which takes 'every creature in, of every kind.' No fastidious delicacy spoils their sports of fancy: though ten times told, the tale to them never can be tedious; though dull 'as the fat weed that grows on Lethe's bank,' the jest for them has all the poignancy of satire: on the very offals, the garbage of wit, they can feed and batten.[85] Happy they who can find in every jester the wit of Sterne or Swift;[86] who else can wade through hundreds of thickly printed pages to obtain for their reward such witticisms as the following: –

'Two Irishmen having travelled on foot from Chester to Barnet, were confoundly tired and fatigued by their journey; and the more so when they were told that they had still about ten miles to go. "By my shoul and St Patrick," cries one of them, "it is but five miles a-piece."'

Here, notwithstanding the promise of a jest held forth by the words, 'By my shoul and St Patrick,' we are ultimately cheated of our hopes. To the ignorant, indeed, the word of promise is kept to the mind as well as to the ear; but others perceive that, instead of a bull, they have only a piece of sentimental arithmetic, founded upon the elegant theorem, that friendship doubles all our pleasures, and divides all our pains.

We must not, from false delicacy to our countrymen, here omit a piece of advice to English retailers or inventors of Irish blunders. Let them beware of such prefatory exclamations as – '*By my shoul and St Patrick! By Jasus! Arrah, honey! My dear joy !*' &c., because all such phrases, beside being absolutely out of date and fashion in Ireland, raise too high an expectation in the minds of a British audience, operating as much to the disadvantage of the story-teller as the dangerous exordium of – 'I'll tell you an excellent story;' an exordium ever to be avoided by all prudent wits.

Another caution should be given to well-meaning ignorance. Never produce that as an Irish bull for which any person of common literature can immediately supply a precedent from our best authors. Never be at the pains, for instance, of telling from Joe Miller, a *good* story of an *Irish* sailor, who *travelled* with Captain Cook[87] *round* the world, and afterwards swore to his companions that it was as flat as a table.

This anecdote, however excellent, immediately finds a parallel in Pope:

> 'Mad Mathesis alone was unconfined,
> Too mad for mere material chains to bind;
> Now to pure space lifts her ecstatic stare,
> Now running *round* the circle finds it square.'[88]

Pope was led into the blunder of representing mad Mathesis running *round the circle*, and finding it *square* by a confused notion that mathematicians had considered the circle as composed of straight lines. His mathematical friends could have told him, that though it was talked of as a polygon, it was not supposed to be square; but *polygon* would not have rhymed to *stare*; and poets, when they launch into the ocean of words, must have an eye to the helm; at all events a poet, who is not supposed to be a student of the exact sciences, may be forgiven for a mathematical blunder. This affair of squaring the circle seems to be peculiarly liable to error; for even an accurate mathematican cannot speak of it without committing something very like a bull.

Dr Hutton, in his Treatise on Mensuration, p. 119, says, 'As the *famous* quadrature of the late Mr John Machin, professor of astronomy in Gresham College, is extremely expeditious and *but little known*, I shall take this opportunity of explaining it.'[89]

It is to be presumed, that the doctor here uses the word *famous* in that acceptation in which it is daily and hourly employed by our Bond-street loungers, by city apprentices, and men of the ton.[90] 'That was a *famous* good joke;' 'He is a *famous* whip;' 'We had a *famous* hop,' &c. Now it cannot be supposed that any of these things are in themselves entitled to fame; but they may, indeed, by the courtesy of England, be at once *famous*, and but little known. It is unnecessary to enter into the defence either of Dr Hutton or of Pope, for they were not born in Ireland, therefore they cannot make bulls; and assuredly their mistakes will not, in the opinion of any person of common sense or candour, derogate from their reputation.

'Never strike till you are sure to wound,' is a maxim well known to the polite* and politic part of the world. 'Never laugh when the laugh can be turned against you,' should be the maxim of those

---

* Lord Chesterfield.[91]

who find their chief pleasure in making others ridiculous. This principle, if applied to our subject, would lead, however, to a very extensive and troublesome system of mutual forbearance; troublesome in proportion to the good or ill humour of the parties concerned, extensive in proportion to their knowledge and acquirements. A man of cultivated parts will foresee the possibility of the retort courteous, where an ignorant man will enjoy the fearless bliss of ignorance. For example, an illiterate person may enjoy a hearty laugh at the common story of an old Irish beggarman, who, pretending to be dumb, was thrown off his guard by the question, 'How many years have you been dumb?' and answered 'Five years last St John's Eve, please your honour.'[92]

But our triumph over the Irishman abates, when we recollect in the History of England, and in Shakspeare, the case of Saunder Simcox, who pretended to be miraculously and instantaneously cured of blindness at St Alban's shrine.[93]

Since we have bestowed so much criticism on the blunder of a beggar-man, a word or two must be permitted on the blunder of a thief. It is natural for ignorant people to laugh at the Hibernian who said that he had stolen a pound of chocolate *to make tea of*. But philosophers are disposed to abstain from the laugh of superiority when they recollect that the Irishman could possibly make as good tea from chocolate as the chemist could make butter, sugar, and cream, from antimony, sulphur, and tartar. The absurdities in the ancient chemical nomenclature could not be surpassed by any in the Hibernian catalogue. If the reader should think this a rash and unwarrantable assertion, we refer him to an essay,* in which the flagrant abuses of speech in the old language of chemistry are admirably exposed and ridiculed. Could an Irishman confer a more

---

* Essay on Chemical Nomenclature, by S. Dickson, M.D.; in which are comprised observations on the same subject, by R. Kirwan, Pres. R.I.A. – Vide pages 21, 22, 23, &c.

appropriate appellation upon a white powder than that of *beautiful black*?

It is really provoking to perceive, that as our knowledge of science or literature extends, we are in more danger of finding, in our own and foreign languages, parallels and precedents for Irish blunders; so that a very well informed man can scarcely with any grace or conscience smile, where a booby squire might enjoy a long and loud horse-laugh of contempt.

What crowds were collected to see the Irish bottle conjuror* get in a quart bottle; but Dr Desaguliers had prepared the English to think such a condensation of animal particles not impossible. He says, vol. i p. 5, of his Lectures on Natural Philosophy, 'that the nature of things should last, and their natural course continue the same; all the changes made in bodies must arise only from the various separations, new conjunctions, and motions, of these original particles. *These must be imagined of an unconceivable smallness*, but by the union of them there are made bigger lumps,' &c.[94]

Indeed things are now come to such a lamentable pass, that without either literary or scientific acquirements, mere local knowledge, such as can be obtained from a finger-post, may sometimes prevent us from the full enjoyment of the Bœotian[95] absurdity of our neighbours. What can, at first view, appear a grosser blunder than that of the Irishman who begged a friend to look over his library, to find for him the history of the world before the creation? Yet this anachronism of ideas is not unparalleled; it is matched, though on a more contracted scale, by an inscription on a British finger-post –

> 'Had you seen these roads before they were made,
> You'd lift up your eyes, and bless Marshal Wade!'[96]

† This conjuror, whose name was Broadstreet, was a native of the county of Longford, in Ireland: he by this hit pocketed 200*l*., and proved himself to be more knave than fool.

The Bliss of Ignorance

There is, however, a rabbi, mentioned by Bayle, who far exceeds both the Irishman and the finger-post. He asserts, that Providence questioned Adam concerning the creation before he was born; and that Adam knew more of the matter than the angels who had laughed at him.[97]

Those who see things in a philosophical light must have observed more frequently than others, that there is in this world, a continual recurrence or rotation of ideas, events, and blunders. With his utmost ingenuity, or his utmost absurdity, a man, in modern days, cannot contrive to produce a system for which there is no prototype in antiquity, or to commit a blunder for which there is no precedent. For example: during the late rebellion in Ireland, at the military execution of some wretched rebel, the cord broke, and the criminal, who had been only half hanged, fell to the ground. The major, who was superintending the execution, exclaimed, 'You rascal, if you do that again, I'll kill you, as sure as you breathe.'

Now this is by no means an original idea. In an old French book, called 'La Charlatanerie des Savans,' is the following note: – 'D'autres ont proposé et résolu en même tems des questions ridicules; par exemple celle-ci: Devroit-on faire souffrir une seconde fois le même genre de mort à un criminel, qui après avoir eu la tête coupée viendroit à réscusciter?' – *Finkelth*, Præf. ad Observationes Pract. num. 12.[98]

The passionate major, instead of being a mere Irish *blunderer*, was, without knowing it, a learned casuist; for he was capable of deciding, in one word, a question, which, it seems, had puzzled the understandings of the ablest lawyers of France, or which had appalled their conscientious sensibility.

Alas, there is nothing new under the sun![99]

'Where ignorance is bliss, 'tis folly to be wise.'[100]

Chapter VI

'Thoughts that Breathe and Words that Burn'

We lamented, in our last chapter, that there is nothing new under the sun; yet, perhaps, the thoughts and phraseology of the following story may not be familiar to the English.

'Plase your honour,' says a man, whose head is bound up with a garter, in token and commemoration of his having been at a fair the preceding night – 'Plase your honour, it's what I am striving since six o'clock and before, this morning, becààse[101] I'd sooner trouble your honour's honour than any man in all Ireland, on account of your cha*ra*cter, and having lived under your family, me and mine, twenty years, aye, say forty again to the back o'that, in the old gentleman's time, as I well remember before I was born; that same time I heard tell of your own honour's riding a little horse in green with your gun before you a grousing over our town-lands, which was the mill and abbey of Ballynagobogg, though 'tis now set away from me (owing to them that belied my father) to Christy Salmon, becààse he's an Orange-man – or his wife – though he was once (let him deny it who can), to *my certain knowledge*, behind the haystack in Tullygore, *sworn in* a United man by captain Alick, who was hanged — Pace to the dead any how! — Well, not to be talking too much of that now, only for this Christy Salmon, I should be still living under your honour.'[102]

'Very likely; but what has all this to do with the present business? If you have any complaint to make against Christy Salmon, make it – if not, let me go to dinner.'

'Oh, it would be too bad to be keeping your honour from your dinner, but I'll make your honour sinsible immadiately. It is not of Christy Salmon at-all-at-all I'm talking. May be your honour is not sinsible yet who I am – I am Paddy M'Doole, of the Curragh, and I've been a flax-dresser and dealer since I parted your honour's land, and was last night at the fair of Clonaghkilty,[103] where I went just in a quiet way thinking of nothing at all, as any man might, and had my little yarn along with me, my wife's and the girl's year's spinning, and all just hoping to bring them back a few honest shillings as they desarved – none better! – Well, plase your honour, my beast lost a shoe, which brought me late to the fair, but not so late but what it was as throng as ever; you could have walked over the heads of the men, women, and childer, a foot and a horseback, all buying and selling; so I to be sure thought no harm of doing the like; so I makes the best bargain I could of the little hanks for my wife and the girl, and the man I sold them to was just weighing them at the crane, and I standing forenent him – "Success to myself!" said I, looking at the shillings I was putting into my waistcoat pocket for my poor family, when up comes the inspector, whom I did not know, I'll take my oath, from Adam, nor couldn't know, becààse he was the deputy inspector, and had been but just made, of which I was ignorant, by this book and all the books that ever were shut and opened – but no matter for that; he seizes my hanks out of the scales that I had just sold, saying they were unlawful and forfeit, becààse by his watch it was past four o'clock, which I denied to be possible, plase your honour, becààse not one, nor two, nor three, but all the town and country were selling the same as myself in broad day, only when the deputy came up they stopped, which I could not, by rason I did not know him. – "Sir," says I (very civil), "if I had known you, it would have been another case, but any how I hope no jantleman will be making it a crime to a poor man to sell his little matter of yarn for his wife and childer after four o'clock, when he did not know it was contrary to law at-all-at-all."

"'I gave you notice that it was contrary to law at the fair of Edgerstown,"[104] said he. – "I axe your pardon, sir," said I, "it was my brother, for I was by." – With that he calls me liar, and what not, and takes a grip* of me, and I a grip of my flax, and he had a shilala† and I had none; so he gave it me over the head, I crying "murder! murder!" and clinging to the scales to save me, and they set a swinging and I with them, plase your honour, till the bame comes down a'top o'the back o'my head, and *kilt* me, as your honour sees.'

'I see that you are alive still, I think.'

'It's not his fault if I am, plase your honour, for he left me for dead, and I am as good as dead still: if it be plasing to your honour to examine my head, you'll be sinsible I'm telling nothing but the truth. Your honour never *seen* a man kilt as I was and am – all which I'm ready (when convanient) to swear before your honour.'‡

The reiterated assurances which this hero gives us of his being killed, and the composure with which he offers to swear to his own assassination and decease, appear rather surprising and ludicrous to those who are not aware that *kilt* is here used in a metaphorical sense, and that it has not the full force of our word killed. But we have been informed by a lady of unquestionable veracity, that she very lately received a petition worded in this manner –

'To the right hon lady E—— P——.

'Humbly showeth;

'That your poor petitioner is now lying dead in a ditch,' &c.

This poor Irish petitioner's expression, however preposterous it sounds, might perhaps be justified, if we were inclined to justify an Irishman by the example, not only of poets comic and tragic, but of prose writers of various nations. The evidence in favour both of the fact and the belief, that people can speak and walk after they are

---

* A gripe or fast hold.
† An oak stick, supposed to be cut from the famous wood of Shilala.[105]
‡ This is nearly verbatim from a late Irish complainant.

'Thoughts that Breathe and Words that Burn'

dead, is attested by stout warriors and grave historians. Let us listen to the solemn voice of a princess, who comes sweeping in the sceptred pall of gorgeous tragedy, to inform us that half herself has buried the other half.

> 'Weep eyes; melt into tears these cheeks to lave:
> One half myself lays t'other in the grave.'*

For six such lines as these Corneille received six thousand livres, and the admiration of the French court and people during the Augustan age of French literature. But an Italian is not content with killing by halves. Here is a man from Italy who goes on fighting, not like Witherington, upon his stumps,[106] but fairly after he is dead.

> 'Nor yet perceived the vital spirit fled,
> But still fought on, nor knew that he was dead.'†

Common sense is somewhat shocked at this single instance of an individual fighting after he is dead; but we shall, doubtless, be reconciled to the idea by the example of a gallant and modern commander, who has declared his opinion, that nothing is more feasible than for a garrison to fight, or at least to surrender, after they are dead, nay, after they are buried. – Witness this public document.

---

* 'Pleurez, pleurez mes yeux et fondez vous en eau,
 La moitié de ma vie a mis l'autre au tombeau.[107]
† 'Il pover uomo che non sen' era accorto,
 Andava combattendo ed erà morto.'[108]

'Liberty and Equality.

'May 29th, 30th Floreal, 6. } Garrison of Ostend.

'Muscar, commandant of Ostend, to the commandant in chief of his British majesty.

'General,

'The council of war was sitting when I received the honour of your letters. We have unanimously resolved not to surrender the place until we shall have been buried in its ruins,' &c.[109]

One step further in hyperbole is reserved for him, who, being buried, carries about his own sepulchre.

> 'To live a life half dead, a living death,
> And buried; but oh, yet more miserable!
> Myself my sepulchre, a moving grave!'[110]

No person, if he heard this passage for the first time from the lips of an Irishman, could hesitate to call it a series of bulls; yet these lines are part of the beautiful complaint of Samson Agonistes on his blindness. Such are the hyperboles sanctioned by the genius, or, what with some judges may have more influence, the name of Milton. The bounds which separate sublimity from bombast, and absurdity from wit, are as fugitive as the boundaries of taste. Only those who are accustomed to examine and appraise literary goods are sensible of the prodigious change that can be made in their apparent value by a slight change in the manufacture. The absurdity of a man's swearing he was killed, or declaring that he is now dead in a ditch, is revolting to common sense; yet the *living death* of Dapperwit, in the 'Rape of the Lock,' is not absurd, but witty; and representing men as dying many times before their death is in Shakspeare sublime:

> 'Cowards die many times before their death;
> The brave can never taste of death but once.'[111]

The most direct contradictions in words do not (*in English writers*) destroy the effect of irony, wit, pathos, or sublimity.

In the classic ode on Eton College, the poet exclaims –

> 'To each their sufferings, all are men,
> Condemn'd alike to groan;
> The feeling for another's pain,
> Th' *unfeeling* for their own.'[112]

Who but a half-witted dunce would ask how those that are unfeeling can have sufferings? When Milton in melodious verse inquires,

> 'Who shall tempt with *wandering feet*
> The dark *unbottom'd* infinite abyss,
> And through the *palpable obscure* find out
> His uncouth way!' —[113]

What Zoilus[114] shall dare interrupt this flow of poetry to object to the palpable obscure, or to ask how feet can wander upon that which has no bottom?

It is easy, as Tully as long ago observed, to fix the brand of ridicule upon the *verbum ardens* of orators and poets – the 'Thoughts that breathe, and words that burn.'[115]

Chapter VII

Practical Bulls

As we have not hitherto been successful in finding original Irish bulls in language, we must now look for them in conduct. A person may be guilty of a solecism without uttering a single syllable – 'That man has been guilty of a solecism with his hand,' an ancient critic said of an actor, who had pointed his hand upwards when invoking the infernal gods.[116] 'You may act a lie as well as speak one,' says Wollaston.[117] Upon the same principle, the Irish may be said to act, as well as to utter bulls. We shall give some instances of their practical bulls, which we hope to find unmatched by the blunders of all other nations. Most people, whether they be savage or civilized, can contrive to revenge themselves upon their enemies without blundering; but the Irish are exceptions. They cannot even do this without *a bull*. During the late Irish rebellion, there was a banker to whom they had a peculiar dislike, and on whom they had vowed vengeance: accordingly they got possession of as many of his banknotes as they could, and made a bonfire of them! This might have been called a feu de joie, perhaps, but certainly not un feu d'artifice; for nothing could show less art than burning a banker's notes in order to destroy his credit. How much better do the English understand the arts of vengeance! Captain Drinkwater* informs us, that during the siege of Gibraltar, the English, being half-famished, were most violently enraged against the Jews, who withheld their stores of provision, and made money of the public distress – a crime *never committed except by Jews*: at length the fleet relieved the

---

* See his account of the siege of Gibraltar.

besieged, and as soon as the fresh provisions were given out, the English soldiers and sailors, to revenge themselves upon the Jews, burst open their stores, and actually roasted a pig at a fire made of cinnamon.[118] There are other persons, as well as the Irish, who do not always understand their own interests where their passions are concerned. That great warrior, Hyder Ali, once lost a battle by a practical bull. Being encamped within sight of the British, he resolved to give them a high idea of his forces and of his artillery; for this purpose, before the engagement,* he ordered his army to march early, and conveying some large pieces of cannon to the top of the hill, he caused them to be pointed at the English camp, which they reached admirably well, and occasioned a kind of disorder and haste in striking and removing tents, &c. Hyder, delighted at having thus insulted the English, caused all his artillery, even the very smallest pieces, to be drawn up the hill for the purpose of making a vain parade, though the greater part of the balls could never reach the English: he imagined he should give the enemy a high idea of his forces, and intimidate them by showing all his artillery, and the vivacity with which it was worked; and in order that his intention might be answered, he encouraged the soldiers himself, by giving money to the cannoneers of those pieces that appeared to be best served.

The English, presently after this farce was over, obliged Hyder to come down from labour-in-vain hill, and to give them battle in earnest. As the historian observes, 'The ridiculous cannonade at the top of the hill had exhausted his ammunition, his great guns were useless to him, and he lost the day by his premature rejoicings before the battle.'[119] A still more ancient precedent for this preposterous practical bull, of rejoicing for an anticipated victory, was given by Xerxes, we believe, who brought with him an immense

---

* Life of Hyder Ali Khan, vol. ii. p. 231.

block of marble, on which he intended to inscribe the date and manner of his victory over the Greeks. When Xerxes was defeated, the Greeks dedicated this stone to Nemesis, the goddess of vengeance. But Xerxes was in the habit of making practical bulls, such as whipping the sea, and begging pardon for it afterwards; throwing fetters into the Hellespont as a token of subjugation, and afterwards expiating his offence by an offering of a golden cup and Persian scimetar.[120]

To such blunders can the passions betray the most renowned heroes, although they had not the misfortune to have been born in Ireland.

The impatience which induced Hyder Ali to anticipate victory is not confined to military men and warlike operations; if we descend to common life and vulgar business, we shall find the same disposition even in the precincts of Change-alley:[121] those who bargained for South Sea stock, that was not actually forthcoming, were called *bears*, in allusion to the practice of the hunters of bears in Canada, who were accustomed to bargain for the skin of the bear before it was caught; but whence the correlative term *bull* is derived we are at a loss to determine, and we must also leave it to the mercantile speculators of England to explain why gentlemen call themselves bulls of wheat and bulls of coals:[122] all we can say is, that these are not Irish bulls. There is one distinguishing peculiarity of the Irish bull – its horns *are tipped with brass*.* It is generally supposed that persons who have been dipped in the Shannon† are ever afterwards endowed with a supernatural portion of what is called by enemies impudence or assurance, by friends, self-possession or *civil courage*. These invulnerable mortals are never oppressed with *mauvaise honte*, that malady which keeps the faculties of the soul under

---

* See the advice of Cleomenes to Crius.
HERODOTUS ERATO.[123]

†It is said that the waters of the Garonne[124] are famed for a similar virtue.

imaginary imprisonment. A well-dipped Irishman, on the contrary, can move, speak, think, like Demosthenes,[125] with as much ease, when the eyes of numbers are upon him, as if the spectators were so many cabbage-stocks. This virtue of *civil courage* is of inestimable value in the opinion of the best judges. The great lord Verulam[126] – no one, by the by, could be a better judge of its value than he, who wanted it so much – the great lord Verulam declares, that if he were asked what is the first, second, and third thing necessary to success in public business, he should answer boldness, boldness, boldness. Success to the nation which possesses it in perfection! Bacon was too accurate and candid a philosopher not to acknowledge, that like all the other goods of life this same boldness has its countervailing disadvantages.

'Certainly,' says he, 'to men of great judgment, bold persons are a sport to behold; nay, and to the vulgar, boldness hath somewhat of the ridiculous; for if absurdity be the subject of laughter, doubt you not but great boldness is seldom without some absurdity; especially it is a sport to see when a bold fellow is out of countenance, for that puts his face into a most shrunken and wooden posture, as needs it must.'[127]

The man, however, who possesses boldness in perfection, can never be put out of countenance, and consequently can never exhibit, for the sport of his enemies, a face in this wooden posture. It is the deficiency, and not the excess of this quality, that is to be feared. Civil boldness without military courage would, indeed, be somewhat ridiculous: but we cannot accuse the Irish of any want of military courage; on the contrary, it is supposed in England, that an Irishman is always ready *to give any gentleman satisfaction*,[128] even when none is desired.

At the close of the American war, as a noble lord of high naval character was returning home to his family after various escapes from danger, he was detained a day at Holyhead[129] by contrary winds. Reading in a summer-house, he heard the well-known sound of bullets whistling near him: he looked about, and found that two balls had just passed through the door close beside him; he looked out of the window, and saw two gentlemen who were just charging their pistols again, and, as he guessed that they had been shooting at a mark upon the door, he rushed out, and very civilly remonstrated with them on the imprudence of firing at the door of a house without having previously examined whether any one was withinside. One of them immediately answered, in a tone which proclaimed at once his disposition and his country, 'Sir, I did not know you were within there, and I don't know who you are now; but if I've given offence, I am willing,' said he, holding out the ready-charged pistols, 'to give you *the satisfaction of a gentleman* – take your choice.'

With his usual presence of mind, the noble lord seized hold of both the pistols, and said to his astonished countryman, 'Do me the justice, sir, to go into that summer-house, shut the door, and let me have two shots at you; then we shall be upon equal terms, and I shall be quite at your service to give or receive the *satisfaction of a gentleman.*'

There was an air of drollery and of superiority in his manner which at once struck and pleased the Hibernian. 'Upon my conscience, sir, I believe you are an honest fellow,' said he, looking him earnestly in the face, 'and I have a great mind to shake hands with you. Will you only just tell me who you are?'

The nobleman told his name – a name dear to every Briton and every Irishman.[130]

'I beg your pardon, and that's what no man ever accused me of doing before,' cried the gallant Hibernian; 'and had I known who you were, I would as soon have *shot my own soul* as have fired at the door. But how could I tell who was withinside?'

'That is the very thing of which I complain,' said his lordship.

His candid opponent admitted the justice of the complaint as soon as he understood it, and he promised never more to be guilty of such a practical bull.

Chapter VIII

The Dublin Shoeblack

Upon looking over our last chapter on practical bulls, we were much concerned to find that we have so few Irish and so many foreign blunders. It is with still more regret we perceive that, notwithstanding our utmost diligence, we have not yet been able to point out the distinguishing characteristic of an Irish bull. But to compensate for this disappointment we have devised a syllogism, which some people may prefer to an à priori argument, to prove irrefragably, that the Irish are blunderers.

After the instances we have produced, chapter 6th, of the *verbum ardens* of English and foreign poets, and after the resemblance that we have pointed out betwixt certain figures of rhetoric and the Irish bull, we have little reason to fear that the candid and enlightened reader should object to our major.[131]

Major. – Those who use figurative language are disposed to make bulls.

Minor. – The Irish use figurative language.

Conclusion. – Therefore the Irish are disposed to make bulls.

We proceed to establish the truth of our minor, and the first evidence we shall call is a Dublin shoeblack. He is not in circumstances peculiarly favourable for the display of figurative language; he is in a court of justice, upon his trial for life or death. A quarrel happened between two shoeblacks, who were playing at what in England is called pitch-farthing, or heads and tails, and in Ireland, head or harp. One of the combatants threw a small paving stone at his opponent, who drew out the knife with which he used to scrape shoes, and plunged it up to the hilt in his companion's breast. It is necessary for our story to say, that near the hilt of this knife was stamped the name of Lamprey, an eminent cutler in Dublin. The shoeblack was brought to trial. With a number of significant gestures, which on his audience had all the powers that Demosthenes ascribes to action, he, in a language not purely attic, gave the following account of the affair to his judge.

'Why, my *lard*, as I was going past the Royal Exchange[132] I meets Billy, "Billy," says I, "will you sky a copper?" "Done," says he, "Done," says I; and done and done's enough between two jantlemen. With that I ranged them fair and even with my hook-em-snivey[133] – up they go. "Music!" says he, "Skulls!" says I; and down they come three brown mazards. "By the holy! you flesh'd 'em," says he. "You lie," says I. With that he ups with a lump of a two year old, and lets drive at me. I outs with my bread-earner, and gives it him up to Lamprey in the bread-basket.'

To make this intelligible to the English, some comments are necessary. Let us follow the text, step by step, and it will afford our readers, as lord Kames says of Blair's Dissertation on Ossian, a delicious morsal of criticism.[134]

As I was going past the Royal Exchange I meets Billy.

In this apparently simple exordium, the scene and the meeting with Billy are brought before the eye by the judicious use of the present tense.

Billy, says I, will you sky a copper?

A copper! genus pro specie! the generic name of copper for the base individual halfpenny.

Sky a copper.

To sky is a new verb, which none but a master hand could have coined: a more splendid metonomy could not be applied upon a more trivial occasion: the lofty idea of raising a metal to the skies is substituted for the mean thought of tossing up a halfpenny. Our orator compresses his hyperbole into a single word. Thus the mind is prevented from dwelling long enough upon the figure to perceive its enormity. This is the perfection of the art. Let the genius of French exaggeration and of eastern hyperbole hide their diminished heads – Virgil is scarcely more sublime.

>'Ingrediturque solo et caput inter nubila condit.'
>'Her feet on earth, her head amidst the clouds.'[135]

Up they go, continues our orator.
Music! says he – Skulls! says I.

Metaphor continually: on one side of an Irish halfpenny there is a harp; this is expressed by the general term music, which is finely contrasted with the word skull.

Down they come, three brown mazards.

Mazards! how the diction of our orator is enriched from the vocabulary of Shakspeare! the word head, instead of being changed for a more general term, is here brought distinctly to the eye by the term mazard, or face, which is more appropriate to his majesty's profile than the word skull or head.

By the holy! you flesh'd 'em, says he.

By the holy! is an oath in which more is meant than meets the ear; it is an ellipsis – an abridgment of an oath. The full formula runs thus – By the holy poker of hell! This instrument is of Irish invention or imagination. It seems a useful piece of furniture in the place for which is it intended, to stir the devouring flames, and thus to increase the torments of the damned. Great judgment is necessary to direct an orator how to suit his terms to his auditors, so as not to shock their feelings either by what is too much above or too much below common life. In the use of oaths, where the passions are warm, this must be particularly attended to, else they lose their effect, and seem more the result of the head than the heart. But to proceed –

By the holy! you flesh'd 'em.

To *flesh* is another verb of Irish coinage; it means, in shoeblack dialect, to touch a halfpenny, as it goes up into the air, with the fleshy part of the thumb, so as to turn it which way you please, and thus to cheat your opponent. What an intricate explanation saved by one word!

You lie, says I.

Here no periphrasis would do the business.

With that he ups with a lump of a two year old, and lets drive at me.

He ups with. – A verb is here formed of two prepositions – a novelty in grammar. Conjunctions, we all know, are corrupted Anglo-Saxon verbs; but prepositions, according to Horne Tooke,[136] derive only from Anglo-Saxon nouns.

All this time it is possible that the mere English reader may not be able to guess what is it that our orator ups with or takes up. He should be apprised, that a lump of a two year old is a middle-sized stone. This is a metaphor, borrowed partly from the grazier's vocabulary, and partly from the arithmetician's vade-mecum. A stone, to come under the denomination of a lump of a two year old, must be to a less stone, as a two year old calf is to a yearling; or it must be to a larger stone than itself, as a two year old calf is to an ox. Here the scholar sees that there must be two statements, one in the rule of three direct, and one in the rule of three inverse, to obtain precisely the thing required; yet the untutored Irishman, without suspecting the necessity of this operose process, arrives at the solution of the problem by some short cut of his own, as he clearly evinces by the propriety of his metaphor. To be sure there seems some incongruity in his throwing this lump of a two year old calf at his adversary. No arm but that of Milo[137] could be strong enough for such a feat. Upon recollection, however, bold as this figure may seem, there are precedents for its use.

'We read in a certain author,' says Beattie, 'of a giant, who, in his wrath, tore off the top of the promontory, and flung it at the enemy; and so huge was the mass, that you might, says he, have seen goats browsing on it as it flew through the air.'[138] Compared with this, our orator's figure is cold and tame.

'*I outs with my bread-earner,*' continues he.

We forbear to comment on *outs with*, because the intelligent critic immediately perceives that it has the same sort of merit ascribed to *ups with*. What our hero dignifies with the name of his bread-earner is the knife with which, by scraping shoes, he earned his bread. Pope's ingenious critic, Mr Warton, bestows judicious praise upon the art with which this poet, in the Rape of the Lock, has used many 'periphrases and uncommon expressions,' to avoid mentioning the name of *scissars*, which would sound too vulgar for epic dignity – fatal engine, forfex, meeting points, &c.[139] Though the metonymy of *bread-earner* for a shoeblack's knife may not equal these in elegance, it perhaps surpasses them in ingenuity.

I gives it him up to Lamprey in the bread-basket. *

Homer is happy in his description of wounds, but this surpasses him in the characteristic choice of circumstance. *Up to Lamprey* gives us at once a complete idea of the length, breadth, and thickness of the wound, without the assistance of the coroner. It reminds us of a passage in Virgil –

* The stomach.

'Cervice orantis *capulo tenus* abdidit ensem.'
'Up to the hilt his shining falchion sheathed.'[140]

Let us now compare the Irish shoeblack's metaphorical language with the sober *slang* of an English blackguard, who, fortunately for the fairness of the comparison, was placed somewhat in similar circumstances.

Lord Mansfield, examining a man who was a witness in the court of King's Bench, asked him what he knew of the defendant.

'Oh, my lord, I knew him. *I was up to him.*'

'Up to him!' says his lordship; 'what do you mean by being up to him?'

'Mean, my lord! why, *I was down upon him.*'

'Up to him, and down upon him!' says his lordship, turning to counsellor Dunning, 'what does the fellow mean?'

'Why, I mean, my lord, as deep as he thought himself, *I stagged him.*'

'I cannot conceive, friend,' says his lordship, 'what you mean by this sort of language; I do not understand it.'

'Not understand it!' rejoined the fellow, with surprise: *'Lord, what a flat you must be!'*

Though he undervalued lord Mansfield, this man does not seem to have been a very bright genius. In his cant words, '*up to him, down upon him, stagged him,*' there are no metaphors; and we confess ourselves to be as great *flats* as his lordship, for we do not understand this sort of language.[141]

'True, no meaning puzzles more than wit,'[142]

as we may see in another English example. Proverbs have been called the wisdom of nations, therefore it is fair to have recourse to them in estimating national abilities. Now there is an old English proverb, 'Tenterten steeple is the cause of Goodwin sands.'

'This proverb,' says Mr Ray,[143] 'is used when an absurd and ridiculous reason is given of any thing in question: an account of the original whereof I find in one of bishop Latimer's sermons in these words – "Mr Moore was once sent with commission into Kent to try out, if it might be, what was the cause of Goodwin's sands, and the shelf which stopped up Sandwich haven. Thither cometh Mr Moore, and calleth all the country before him, such as were thought to be men of experience, and men that could, of all likelihood, best satisfy him of the matter concerning the stopping of Sandwich haven.[144] Among the rest came in before him an old man with a white head, and one that was thought to be little less than a hundred years old. When Mr Moore saw this aged man, he thought it expedient to hear him say his mind in this matter (for being so old a man, it was likely that he knew the most in that presence or company); so Mr Moore called this old aged man unto him, and said, "Father," said he, "tell me, if you can, what is the cause of the great arising of the sands and shelves hereabout this haven, which stop it up so that no ships can arrive here. You are the oldest man I can espy in all the company, so that if any man can tell any cause of it, you, of all likelihood, can say most to it, or, at leastwise, more than any man here assembled."

'"Yea, forsooth, good Mr Moore," quoth this old man, "for I am well nigh a hundred years old, and no man here in this company any thing near my age."

'"Well, then," quoth Mr Moore, "how say you to this matter? What think you to be the cause of these shelves and sands which stop up Sandwich haven?"

'"Forsooth, sir," quoth he, "I am an old man, I think that Tenterten steeple is the cause of Goodwin's sands. For I am an old man, sir," quoth he, "I may remember the buildings of Tenterten steeple, and I may remember when there was no steeple at all there; and before that Tenterten or *Totterden* steeple was in building, there was no manner of talking of any flats or sands that stopped up the haven, and therefore I think that Tenterton steeple is the cause of the decay and destroying of Sandwich haven.'"* – Thus far the bishop.

The prolix pertinacity with which this *old aged* man adheres to the opinion that he had formed, without any intelligible reason, is characteristic of an English peasant; but however absurd his mode of judging may be, and however confused and incongruous his ideas, his species of absurdity surely bears no resemblance to an Hibernian blunder. We cannot even suspect it to be possible that a man of this slow, circumspect character could be in any danger of making an Irish bull; and we congratulate the English peasantry and populace, as a body, upon their possessing that temper which

> 'Wisely rests content with sober sense,
> Nor makes to dangerous wit a vain pretence.'[145]

Even the *slang* of English pickpockets and coiners is, as we may see in Colquhoun's *View of the Metropolis*, free from all seducing mixture of wit and humour. What Englishman would ever have thought of calling persons in the pillory *the babes in the wood*? This is a common cant phrase amongst Dublin reprobates. Undoubtedly such phrases tend to lessen the power of shame and the effect of punishment, and a witty rogue will lead numbers to the gallows. English morality is not in so much danger as Irish manners must be from these humorous talents in their knights of industry. If, nevertheless, there be frequent executions for capital crimes in England, we must account for this in the words of the old lord chief

---

* This ancient old man, we fear, was more knave than fool. History informs us, that the bishop of Rochester had directed the revenue, appropriated for keeping Goodwin harbour in repair, to the purpose of building a steeple. – Vide Fuller's Worthies of England, page 65.[146]

justice Fortescue – 'More men,' says his lordship, 'are hanged in *Englonde* in one year then *in Fraunce* in seven, *because the English have better hartes*; the *Scotchmenne* likewise never *dare rob*, but only commit larcenies.'[147] At all events, the phlegmatic temper of *Englonde* secures her from making bulls. The propensity to this species of blunder exists in minds of a totally different cast; in those who are quick and enthusiastic, who are confounded by the rapidity and force with which undisciplined multitudes of ideas crowd for utterance. Persons of such intellectual characters are apt to make elisions in speaking which, they trust, the capacities of their audience will supply: passing rapidly over a long chain of thought, they sometimes forget the intermediate links, and no one but those of equally rapid habits can follow them successfully.

We hope that the evidence of the Dublin shoeblack has, in some degree, tended to prove our *minor*, that the Irish are disposed to use figurative language: we shall not, however, rest our cause on a single evidence, however respectable; but before we summon our other witnesses, we beg to relieve the reader's attention, which must have been fatigued by such a chapter of criticism. They shall now have the tale of a mendicant. A specimen of city rhetoric is given in the shoeblack; the country mendicant's eloquence is of a totally different species.

Chapter IX

The Hibernian Mendicant

Perhaps the reader may wish to see as well as hear the petitioner. At first view you might have taken him for a Spaniard. He was tall; and if he had been a gentleman, you would have said that there was an air of dignity in his figure. He seemed very old, yet he appeared more worn by sorrow than by time. Leaning upon a thick oaken stick as he took off his hat to ask for alms, his white hair was blown by the wind.

'Health and long life to you!' said he. 'Give an old man something to help to bury him. He is past his labour, and cannot trouble this world long any way.'

He held his hat towards us, with nothing importunate in his manner, but rather with a look of confidence in us, mixed with habitual resignation. His thanks were: 'Heaven bless you! – Long life and success to you! to you and yours! and may you never want a friend, as I do.'

The last words were spoken low. He laid his hand upon his heart as he bowed to us, and walked slowly away. We called him back; and upon our questioning him farther, he gave the following account of himself: –

'I was bred and born – but no matter where such a one as I was bred and born, no more than where I may die and be buried. *I*, that have neither son, nor daughter, nor kin, nor friend, on the wide earth, to mourn over my grave when I am laid in it, as I soon must. Well! when it pleases God to take me, I shall never be missed out of this world, so much as by a dog and why should I? Having never in my time done good to any – but evil – which I have lived to repent me of, many's the long day and night, and ever shall whilst I have sense and reason left. In my youthful days God was too good to me: I had friends, and a little home of my own to go to – a pretty spot of land for a farm, as you could see, with a snug cabin, and every thing complete, and all to be mine; for I was the only one my father and mother had, and accordingly was made much of, too much; for I grew headstrong upon it, and high, and thought nothing of any man, and little of any woman, but one. That one I surely did think of; and well worth thinking of she was. Beauty, they say, is all fancy; but she was a girl every man might fancy. Never was one more sought after. She was then just in her prime, and full of life and spirits; but nothing light in her behaviour – quite modest – yet obliging. She was too good for me to be thinking of, no doubt; but "faint heart never won fair lady,"[148] so I made bold to speak to Rose, for that was her name, and after a world of pains, I began to gain upon her good liking, but couldn't get her to say more than that she never *seen* the man she should fancy so well. This was a great deal from her, for she was coy and proud-like, as she had a good right to be; and, besides being young, loved her little innocent pleasure, and could not *easy* be brought to give up her sway. No fault of hers: but all very natural. Well! I always considered she never would have held out so long, nor have been so stiff with me, had it not been for an old aunt Honour of hers – God rest her soul! One should not be talking ill of the dead; but she was more out of my way than enough; yet the cratur had no malice in her against me, only meaning her child's good, as she called it, but mistook it, and thought to make Rose happy by some greater match than me, counting her fondness for me, which she could not but see something of, childishness, that she would soon be broke of. Now there was a party of English soldiers quartered in our town, and there was a sergeant amongst them that had money, and a pretty place, as they said, in his own country. He courted Rose, and the aunt favoured him. He and I could never relish one another at all. He was a handsome portly man, but very proud, and looked upon me as dirt under his feet, because I was an Irishman; and at every word would say, "*That's an Irish bull!*" or, "*Do you hear Paddy's brogue?*" at which his fellow-soldiers, being all English, would look greatly delighted. Now all this I could have taken in good part from any but him, for I was not an ill-humoured fellow; but there was a spite in him I plainly saw against me, and I could not, nor would not take a word from him against me or my country, especially when Rose was by, who did not like me the worse for having a proper spirit. She little thought what would come of it. Whilst all this was going on, her aunt Honour found to object against me, that I was wild, and given to drink; both which charges were false and malicious, and I knew could come from none other than the sergeant, which enraged me the more against him for speaking *so mean* behind my back. Now I knew, that though the sergeant did not drink spirits, he drank plenty of beer. Rose took it, however, to heart, and talked very serious upon it, observing she could never think to marry a man given to drink, and that the sergeant was remarkably sober and staid, therefore most like, as her aunt Honour said, to make a good husband. The words went straight to my heart, along with Rose's look. I said not a word, but went out, resolving, before I slept, to take an oath against spirits of all sorts for Rose's sweet sake. That evening I fell in with some boys of the neighbours, who would have had me along with them, but *I denied myself* and them; and all I would taste was one parting glass, and then made my vow in the presence of the priest, forswearing spirits for two years. Then I went straight to her house to tell her what I had done, not being sensible that I was that same time a little elevated with the parting glass I had taken. The first thing I noticed on going into the room was the man I least wished to see there, and least looked for at this minute: he was in high talk with the aunt, and Rose sitting on the other side of him, no way strange towards him, as I fancied; but

The Hibernian Mendicant

that was only fancy, and effect of the liquor I had drunk, which made me see things wrong. I went up, and put my head between them, asking Rose, did she know what I had been about?

"'Yes; too well!' said she, drawing back from my breath. And the aunt looked at her, and she at the aunt, and the sergeant stopped his nose, saying he had not been long enough in Ireland to love the smell of whiskey. I observed, that was an uncivil remark in the present company, and added, that I had not taken a drop that night, but one glass. At which he sneered, and said that was a bull and a blunder, but no wonder, as I was an Irishman. I replied in defence of myself and country. We went on from one smart word to another; and some of his soldiermen being of the company, he had the laugh against me still. I was vexed to see Rose bear so well what I could not bear myself. And the talk grew higher and higher; and from talking of blunders and such trifles, we got, I cannot myself tell you how, on to great party matters, and politics, and religion. And I was a catholic, and he a protestant; and there he had the thing still against me. The company seeing matters not agreeable, dropped off till none were left but the sergeant, and the aunt, and Rose, and myself. The aunt gave me a hint to part, but I would not take it; for I could not bear to go away worsted, and borne down as it were by the English faction, and Rose by to judge. The aunt was called out by one who wanted her to go to a funeral next day: the Englishman then let fall something about our Irish howl, and savages, which Rose herself said was uncivil, she being an Irish woman, which he, thinking only of making game on me, had forgot. I knocked him down, telling him that it was he that was the savage to affront a lady. As he got up he said that he'd have the law of me, if any law was to be had in Ireland.

"'The law!' said I, "and you a soldier!"

"'Do you mean to call me coward?' said he. "This is what an English soldier must not bear." With that he snatches at his arms that were beside him, asking me again, did I mean to call an Englishman coward?

"'Tell me first,' said I, 'did you mean to call us Irish savages?'"

"'That's no answer to *my* question,' says he, 'or only an Irish answer.'"

"'It is not the worse for that, may be,' says I, very coolly, despising the man now, and just took up a knife, that was on the table, to cut off a button that was hanging at my knee. As I was opening of the knife he asks me, was I going to stab at him with my Irish knife, and directly fixes a bayonet at me; on which I seizes a musket and bayonet one of his men had left, telling him I knew the use of it as well as he or any Englishman, and better; for that I should never have gone, as he did, to charge it against an unarmed man.

"'You had your knife,' said he, drawing back.

"'If I had, it was not thinking of you,' said I, throwing the knife away. 'See! I'm armed like yourself now: fight me like a man and a soldier, if you dare,' says I.

"'Fight me, if you dare,' says he.

Rose calls to me to stop; but we were both out of ourselves at the minute. We thrust at each other – he missed me –I hit him. Rose ran in between us to get the musket from my hand: it was loaded, and went off in the struggle, and the ball lodged in her body. She fell! and what happened next I cannot tell, for the sight left my eyes, and all sense forsook me. When I came to myself the house was full of people, going to and fro, some whispering, some crying; and, till the words reached my ears, 'Is she quite dead?' I could not understand where I was, or what had happened. I wished to forget again, but could not. The whole truth came upon me, and yet I could not shed a tear! but just pushed my way through the crowd into the inner room, and up to the side of the bed. There she lay stretched, almost a corpse – quite still! Her sweet eyes closed, and no colour in her cheeks, that had been so rosy! I took hold of one of her hands, that hung down, and she then opens her eyes, and knew me directly, and smiles upon me, and says, 'It was no fault of yours: take notice, all of you, it was no fault of his if I die; but *that* I won't do for his sake, if I can help it!' – that was the word she spoke. I thinking, from her speaking so strong, that she was not badly hurt, knelt down to whisper to her, that if my breath did smell of spirits, it was the parting glass I had tasted before making the vow I had done against drink for her sake; and that there was nothing I would not do for her, if it would please God to spare her to me. She just pressed my hand, to show me she was sensible. The priest came in, and they forced our hands asunder, and carried me away out of the room. Presently there was a great cry, and I knew all was over.'

Here the old man's voice failed, and he turned his face from us. When he had somewhat recovered himself, to change the course of his thoughts, we asked whether he were prosecuted for his assault on the English sergeant, and what became of him?

'Oh! to do him justice, as one should do to every one,' said the old man, 'he behaved very handsome to me when I was brought to trial; and told the whole truth, only blamed himself more than I would have done, and said it was all his fault for laughing at me and my nation more than a man could bear, situated as I was. They acquitted me through his means. We shook hands, and he hoped all would go right with me, he said; but nothing ever went right with me after. I took little note ever after of worldly matters: all belonging to me went to rack and ruin. The hand of God was upon me: I could not help myself, nor settle mind or body to any thing. I heard them say sometimes I was a little touched in my head: however that might be I cannot say. But at the last I found it was as good for me to give all that was left to my friends, who were better able to manage, and more eager for it than I; and fancying a roving life would agree with me best, I quit the place, taking nothing with me, but resolved to walk the world, and just trust to the charity of good christians, or die, as it should please God. How I have lived so long He only knows, and his will be done.'

Chapter X

Irish Wit and Eloquence

'Wild wit, invention ever new,'[149] appear in high perfection amongst even the youngest inhabitants of an Irish cottage. The word wit, amongst the lower classes in Ireland, means not only quickness of repartee, but cleverness in action; it implies invention and address, with no slight mixture of cunning; all which is expressed in their dialect by the single word '*cuteness* (acuteness). Examples will give a better notion of this than can be conveyed by any definition.

An Irish boy (a 'cute lad) saw a train of his companions leading their cars, loaded with kishes* of turf, coming towards his father's cabin; his father had no turf, and the question was how some should be obtained. To beg he was ashamed; to dig he was unwilling – but his head went to work directly. He took up a turf which had fallen from one of the cars the preceding day, and stuck it on the top of a pole near the cabin. When the cars were passing, he appeared throwing turf at the mark. 'Boys!' cried he 'which of ye will hit?' Each leader of the car, as he passed, could not forbear to fling a turf at the mark; the turf fell at the foot of the pole, and when all the cars had passed, there was a heap left sufficient to reward the ingenuity of our little Spartan.

The same 'cuteness which appears in youth continues and improves in old age. When general V—— was quartered in a small town in Ireland, he and his lady were regularly besieged, whenever they got into their carriage, by an old beggar-woman, who kept her post at the door, assailing them daily with fresh importunities and fresh tales of distress. At last the lady's charity, and the general's

* Baskets.

patience, were nearly exhausted, but their petitioner's wit was still in its pristine vigour. One morning, at the accustomed hour, when the lady was getting into her carriage, the old woman began – 'Agh! my lady; success to your ladyship, and success to your honour's honour, this morning, of all days in the year; for sure didn't I dream last night that her ladyship gave me a pound of tea, and that your honour gave me a pound of tobacco?'

'But, my good woman,' said the general, 'do not you know that dreams always go by the rule of contrary?'

'Do they so, plase your honour?' rejoined the old woman. 'Then it must be your honour that will give me the tea, and her ladyship that will give me the tobacco?'

The general being of Sterne's opinion, that a bon-mot is always worth more than a pinch of snuff, gave the ingenious dreamer the value of her dream.[150]

Innumerable instances might be quoted of the Hibernian genius, not merely for repartee, but for what the Italians call pasquinade. We shall cite only one, which is already so well known in Ireland, that we cannot be found guilty of *publishing* a libel. Over the ostentatious front of a nobleman's house in Dublin, the owner had this motto cut in stone: –

'Otium cum dignitate. – Leisure with dignity.'[151]

In process of time his lordship changed his residence; or, since we must descend to plebeian language, was committed to Newgate, and immediately there appeared over the front of his apartment his chosen motto, as large as the life, in white chalk,

Otium cum dignitate.

Mixed with keen satire, the Irish often show a sort of cool good sense and dry humour, which gives not only effect, but value to their impromptus. Of this class is the observation made by the Irish hackney coachman, upon seeing a man of the ton driving four-in-hand down Bond-street.[152]

'That fellow,' said our observer, 'looks like a coachman, but drives like a gentleman.'

As an instance of humour mixed with sophistry, we beg the reader to recollect the popular story of the Irishman who was run over by a troop of horse, and miraculously escaped unhurt.

'Down upon your knees and thank God, you reprobate,' said one of the spectators.

'Thank God! for what? Is it for letting a troop of horse run over me?'

In this speech there is the same sort of humour and sophistry that appears in the Irishman's celebrated question: 'What has posterity done for me, that I should do so much for posterity?'[153]

The Irish nation, from the highest to the lowest, in daily conversation about the ordinary affairs of life, employ a superfluity of wit and metaphor which would be astonishing and unintelligible to a majority of the respectable body of English yeomen. Even the cutters of turf and drawers of whiskey are orators;[154] even the *cottiers* and *gossoons*[155] speak in trope and figure. Ask an Irish gossoon to go early in the morning, on an errand, and he answers,

'I'll be off at the flight of night.'

If an Irish cottager would express to his landlord that he wishes for a long lease of his land, he says

'I would be proud to live on your honour's land as long as grass grows or water runs.'

One of our English poets has nearly the same idea: –

> 'As long as streams in silver mazes run,
> Or Spring with annual green renews the grove.'[156]

Without the advantages of a classical education, the lower Irish sometimes make similes that bear a near resemblance to those of the admired poets of antiquity. A loyalist, during the late rebellion, was describing to us the number of the rebels who had gathered on one spot, and were dispersed by the king's army; rallied, and were again put to flight.

'They were,' said he, 'like swarms of flies on a summer's day, that you brush away with your hand, and still they will be returning.'

There is a simile of Homer's which, literally translated, runs thus: 'As the numerous troops of flies about a shepherd's cottage in the Spring, when the milk moistens the pails, such numbers of Greeks stood in the field against the Trojans.'[157] Lord Kames observes, that it is false taste to condemn such comparisons for the lowness of the images introduced. In fact, great objects cannot be degraded by comparison with small ones in these similes, because the only point of resemblance is number; the mind instantly perceives this, and therefore requires no other species of similitude.[158]

When we attempt to judge of the genius of the lower classes of the people, we must take care that we are not under the influence of any prejudice of an aristocratic or literary nature. But this is no easy effort of liberality.

'*Agh! Dublin, sweet Jasus be wid you!*' exclaimed a poor Irishman, as he stood on the deck of a vessel, which was carrying him out of the bay of Dublin. The pathos of this poor fellow will not probably affect delicate sensibility, because he says *wid* instead of *with*, and *Jasus* instead of *Jesus*. Adam Smith is certainly right in his theory, that the sufferings of those in exalted stations have generally most power to command our sympathy.[159] The very same sentiment of sorrow at leaving his country, which was expresed so awkwardly by the poor Irishman, appears, to every reader of taste, exquisitely pathetic from the lips of Mary queen of Scots.[160]

'Farewell, France! Farewell, beloved country! which I shall never more behold!'*

In anger as well as in sorrow the Irishman is eloquent. A gentleman who was lately riding through the county of———, in Ireland, to canvass, called to ask a vote from a poor man, who was planting willows in a little garden by the road side.[161]

'You have a vote, my good sir, I am told,' said the candidate, in an insinuating tone.

The poor man struck the willow which he had in his hand into the ground, and with a deliberate pace came towards the candidate to parley with him.

'Please your honour,' said he gravely, 'I have a vote, and I have not a vote.'

'How can that be?'

'I will tell you, sir,' said he, leaning, or rather lying down slowly upon the back of the ditch[162] facing the road, so that the gentleman, who was on horseback, could see only his head and arms.

'Sir,' said he, 'out of this little garden, with my five acres of land and my own labour, I once had a freehold; but I have been robbed of my freehold, and who do you think has robbed me? why, that man!' pointing to his landlord's steward, who stood beside the candidate. 'With my own hands I sowed my own ground with oats, and a fine crop I expected – but I never reaped that crop: not a bushel, no, nor half a bushel, did I ever see; for into my little place comes this man, with I don't know how many more, with their shovels and their barrows, and their horses and their cars, and to work they fell, and they ran a road straight through the best part of my land, turning all to heaps of rubbish, and a bad road it was, and a bad time of year to make it! But where was *I* when he did this? not where I am now,' said the orator, raising himself up and standing

---

* Vide Robertson's *History of Scotland*.

firm, 'not as you see me now, but lying on my back in my bed in a fever. When I got up, I was not able to make my rent out of my land. Besides myself, I had my five children to support. I sold my clothes, and have never been able to buy any since but such as a recruit could sell, who was in haste to get into regimentals – such clothes as these,' said he, looking down at his black rags. 'Soon I had nothing to eat: but that's not all. I am a weaver, sir: for my rent they seized my two looms; then I had nothing to do. But of all this I do not complain. There was an election some time ago in this county, and a man rode up to me in this garden as you do now, and asked me for my vote, but I refused him, for I was steady to my landlord. The gentleman observed I was a poor man, and asked if I wanted for nothing? but all did not signify; so he rode on gently, and at the corner of the road, within view of my garden, I saw him drop a purse, and I knew, by his looking at me, it was on purpose for me to pick it up. After a while he came back, thinking, to be sure, I had taken up the purse, and had changed my mind, but he found his purse where he left it. My landlord knew all this, and he promised to see justice done me, but he forgot. Then as for the candidate's lady, before the election nothing was too fair-speaking for me; but afterward, in my distress, when I applied to her to get me a loom, which she could have had from *the Linen Board*[163] by only asking for it, her answer to me was, "I don't know that I shall ever want a vote again in the county."

'Now, sir,' continued he, 'when justice is done to me (and no sooner), I shall be glad to assist my landlord or his friend. I know who *you* are, sir, very well: you bear a good character: success to you! but I have no vote to give to you or any man.'

'If I were to attempt to make you any amends for what you have suffered,' replied the candidate, 'I should do you an injury; it would be said that I had bribed you; but I will repeat your story where it will meet with attention. I cannot, however, tell it so well as you have told it.'

'No, sir,' was his answer, 'for you cannot feel it as I do.'

This is almost in terms the conclusion of Pope's epistle from Eloisa to Abelard: –

'He best can paint them who shall feel them most.'[164]

In objurgation and pathetic remonstrancing eloquence, the females of the lower class in Ireland are not inferior to the men. A thin tall woman wrapped in a long cloak, the hood of which was drawn over her head, and shaded her pale face, came to a gentleman to complain of the cruelty of her landlord.

'He is the most hard-hearted man alive, so he is, sir,' said she; 'he has just seized all I have, which, God knows, is little enough! and has driven my cow to pound, the only cow I have, and only dependance I have for a drop of milk to drink; and the cow itself too standing there starving in the pound, for not a wisp of hay would he give to cow or christian to save their lives, if it was ever so! And the rent for which he is driving me,[165] please your honour, has not been due but one week: a hard master he is; but these *middle men*[166] are all so, one and all. Oh! if it had but been my lot to be tenant to a *gentleman born*, like your honour, who is the poor man's friend, and the orphan's, and the widow's – the friend of them that have none other. Long life to you! and long may you live to reign over us! Would you but speak three words to my landlord, to let my cow out of pound, and give me a fortnight's time, that I might see and fatten her to sell against the fair, I could pay him then all honestly, and not be racked[167] entirely, and he would be ashamed to refuse your honour, and afraid to disoblige the like of you, or get your ill-will. May the blessing of Heaven be upon you, if you'll just send and speak to him three words for the poor woman and widow, that has none other to speak for her in the wide world.'

Irish Wit and Eloquence

Moved by this lamentable story, the effect of which the woman's whole miserable appearance corroborated and heightened, the gentleman sent immediately for her hard-hearted landlord. The landlord appeared; not a gentleman, not a rich man, as the term landlord might denote, but a stout, square, stubbed, thick-limbed, gray-eyed man, who seemed to have come smoking hot from hard labour. The gentleman repeated the charge made against him by the poor widow, and mildly remonstrated on his cruelty: the man heard all that was said with a calm but unmoved countenance.

'And now have you done?' said he, turning to the woman, who had recommenced her lamentations. 'Look at her standing there, sir. It's easy for her to put on her long cloak, and to tell her long story, and to make her poor mouth[168] to your honour; but if you are willing to hear, I'll tell you what she is, and what I am. She is one that has none but herself in this world to provide for; she is one that is able to afford herself a glass of whiskey when she pleases, and she pleases it often; she is one that never denies herself the bit of *staggering bob** when in season; she is one that has a snug house well thatched to live in all the year round, and nothing to do or nothing that she does, and this is the way of her life, and this is what she is. And what am I? I am the father of eight children, and I have a wife and myself to provide for. I am a man that is at hard labour of one kind of another from sunrise to sunset. The straw that thatched the house she lives in I brought two miles on my back; the walls of the house she lives in I built with my own hands; I did the same by five other houses, and they are all sound and dry, and good to live in, summer or winter. I set them for rent to put bread into my children's mouth, and after all I cannot get it! And to support my eight children, and my wife, and myself, what have I in this world,' cried he, striding suddenly with colossal firmness upon his sturdy

---

* Slink calf.[169]

legs, and raising to heaven arms which looked like fore-shortenings of the limbs of Hercules, 'what have *I* in this wide world but these four bones?'*

No provocation could have worked up a phlegmatic English countryman to this pitch of eloquence. He never suffers his anger to evaporate in idle figures of speech: it is always concentrated in a few words, which he repeats in reply to every argument, persuasive or invective, that can be employed to irritate or to assuage his wrath. We recollect having once been present at a scene between an English gentleman and a churchwarden, whose feelings were grievously hurt by the disturbance that had been given to certain bones in levelling a wall which separated the churchyard from the pleasure ground of the lord of the manor. The bones belonged, as the churchwarden believed or averred, to his great great grandmother, though how they were identified it might be difficult to explain to an indifferent judge; yet we are to suppose that the confirmation of the suspicion was strong and satisfactory to the party concerned. The pious great great grandson's feelings were all in arms, but *indignation* did not inspire him with a single poetic idea or expression. In his eloquence, indeed, there was the principal requisite, action: in reply to all that could be said, he repeatedly struck his long oak stick perpendicularly upon the floor, and reiterated these words –

'It's death, sir! death by the law! It's sacrilege, sir! sacrilege by act of parliament! It's death, sir! death by the law! and the law I'll have of him, for it's lawful to have the law.'

This was the whole range of his ideas, even when the passions had tumbled them all out of their dormitories.

Innumerable fresh instances of Irish eloquence and wit crowd upon our recollection, but we forbear. The examples we have cited are taken from real life, and given without alteration or embellishment.

---

* This was written down a few minutes after it had been spoken.

Chapter XI

The Brogue

Having proved by a perfect syllogism that the Irish must blunder, we might rest satisfied with our labours; but there are minds of so perverse a sort, that they will not yield their understandings to the torturing power of syllogism.[170]

It may be waste of time to address ourselves to persons of such a cast; we shall therefore change our ground, and adapt our arguments to the level of vulgar capacities. Much of the comic effect of Irish bulls, or of such speeches as are mistaken for bulls, has depended upon the tone, or *brogue*, as it is called, with which they are uttered. The first Irish blunders that we hear are made or repeated in this peculiar tone, and afterward, from the power of association, whenever we hear the tone we expect the blunder. Now there is little danger that the Irish should be cured of their brogue; and consequently there is no great reason to apprehend that we should cease to think or call them blunderers.

Of the powerful effect of any peculiarity of pronunciation to prepossess the mind against the speaker, nay even to excite dislike amounting to antipathy, we have an instance attested by an eye-witness, or rather an ear-witness.

'In the year 1755,' says the Rev. James Adams, 'I attended a public disputation in a foreign university, when at least 400 Frenchmen literally hissed a grave and learned *English* doctor, not by way of insult, but irresistibly provoked by the quaintness of the repetition of sh. The thesis was, the concurrence of God *in actionibus viciosis*: the whole hall resounded with the hissing cry of *sh*, and its continual occurrence in *actio, actione, viciosa*, &c.[171]

It is curious that Shiboleth[172] should so long continue a criterion among nations!

What must have been the degree of irritation that could so far get the better of the politeness of 400 Frenchmen as to make them hiss in the days of *l'ancien regime!* The dread of being the object of that species of antipathy or ridicule which is excited by unfashionable peculiarity of accent has induced many of the *misguided* natives of Ireland to affect what they imagine to be the English pronunciation. They are seldom successful in this attempt, for they generally overdo the business. We are told by Theophrastus, that a *barbarian*, who had taken some pains to attain the true attic dialect, was discovered to be a foreigner by his speaking the attic dialect with a greater degree of precision and purity than was usual amongst the Athenians themselves.[173] To avoid the imputation of committing barbarisms, people sometimes run into solecisms,[174] which are yet more ridiculous. Affectation is always more ridiculous than ignorance.

There are Irish ladies, who, ashamed of their country, betray themselves by mincing out their abjuration, by calling tables *teebles*, and chairs *cheers!* To such renegadoes we prefer the honest quixotism of a modern champion* for the Scottish accent, who, boldly asserting that 'the broad dialect rises above reproach, scorn, and laughter,' enters the lists, as he says of himself, in Tartan dress and armour, and throws down the gauntlet to the most prejudiced antagonist. 'How weak is prejudice!' pursues this patriotic enthusiast. 'The sight of the Highland kelt, the flowing plaid, the buskined leg, provokes my antagonist to laugh! Is this dress ridiculous in the eyes of reason and common sense? No: nor is the dialect of speech: both are characteristic and national distinctions.'[175]

---

* James Adams, S.R.E.S., author of a book entitled, 'The Pronunciation of the English Language vindicated from imputed Anomaly and Caprice; with an Appendix on the Dialects of Human Speech in all Countries, and an analytical Discussion and Vindication of the Dialect of Scotland.'

'The arguments of general vindication,' continues he, 'rise powerful before my sight, like the Highland bands in full array. A louder strain of apologetic speech swells my words. What if it should rise high as the unconquered summits of Scotia's hills, and call back, with voice sweet as Caledonian song, the days of ancient Scottish heroes; or attempt the powerful speech of the Latian orator, or his of Greece! The subject, methinks, would well accord with the attempt: *Cupidum, Scotia optima, vires deficiunt.*[176] I leave this to the *king of songs.* Dunbar and Dunkeld, Douglas in *Virgilian* strains, and later poets, Ramsay, Ferguson, and Burns, awake from your graves; you have already immortalized the Scotch dialect in raptured melody![177] Lend me your golden target and well-pointed spear, that I may victoriously pursue, to the extremity of South Britain, reproachful ignorance and scorn still lurking there: – let impartial candour seize their usurped throne. Great then is the birth of this national dialect,' &c.[178]

So far so good. We have some sympathy with the rhapsodist, whose enthusiasm kindles at the names of Allan Ramsay and of Burns: nay, we are willing to hear (with a grain of allowance) that 'the manly eloquence of the Scotch bar affords a singular pleasure to the candid English hearer, and gives merit and dignity to the noble speakers, who retain so much of their own dialect and tempered propriety of English sounds, that they may be emphatically termed *British orators.*'[179] But we confess that we lose our patient decorum, and are almost provoked to laughter, when our philological Quixote seriously sets about to prove that Adam and Eve spoke broad Scotch in Paradise.

How angry has this grave patriot reason to be with his ingenious countryman Beattie,* the celebrated champion of *Truth*, who acknowledges that he never could, when a boy or man, look at a certain

---

* Vide Illustrations on Sublimity, in his Essays.[180]

translation of Ajax's speech into one of the vulgar Scotch dialects without laughing!

We shall now with boldness, similar to that of the Scotch champion, try the risible muscles of our English reader; we are not, indeed, inclined to go quite such lengths as he has gone: he insists, that the Scotch dialect ought to be adopted all over England; we are only going candidly to confess, that we think the Irish, in general, speak *better English* than is commonly spoken by the natives of England. To limit this proposition so as to make it appear less absurd, we should observe, that we allude to the lower classes of the people in both countries. In some counties of Ireland, a few of the poorest labourers and cottagers do not understand English, they speak only Irish, as in Wales there are vast numbers who speak only Welsh; but amongst those who speak English we find fewer vulgarisms than amongst the same rank of persons in England. The English which they speak is chiefly such as has been traditional in their families from the time of the early settlers in the island. During the reign of Elizabeth and the reign of Shakspeare, numbers of English migrated to Ireland; and whoever attends to the phraseology of the lower Irish may, at this day, hear many of the phrases and expressions used by Shakspeare. Their vocabulary has been preserved nearly in its pristine purity since that time, because they have not had intercourse with those counties in England which have made for themselves a jargon unlike to any language under heaven. The Irish *brogue* is a great and shameful defect, but it does not render the English language absolutely unintelligible. There are but a few variations of the brogue, such as the long and the short, the Thady brogue and Paddy brogue,[181] which differ much in tone, and but little in phraseology; but in England, almost all of our fifty-two counties have peculiar vulgarisms, dialects, and brogues, unintelligible to their neighbours. Herodotus tells us that some of the nations of Greece, though they used the same language, spoke it so differently, that they could not understand each other's conversation.[182] This is literally the case at present between the provincial inhabitants of remote parts of England. Indeed the language peculiar to the metropolis, or the *cockney* dialect, is proverbially ridiculous. The Londoners, who look down with contempt upon all that have not been *bred and born* within the sound of Bow, talk with unconscious absurdity of *w*eal and *w*inegar, and *v*ine and *v*indors, and ide*a*rs, and ask you o*w* you do? and '*ave ye bin taking* the *h*air in 'yde park? and '*as* your 'orse 'ad any *h*oats, &c? aspirating always where they should not, and never aspirating where they should.

The *Zummerzetzheer* dialect, full of broad *oos* and eternal *zeds*, supplies never-failing laughter when brought upon the stage. Even a cockney audience relishes the broad pronunciation of John Moody, in the *Journey to London*, or of Sim, in *Wild Oats*.[183]

The cant of Suffolk, the vulgarisms of Shropshire, the uncouth phraseology of the three ridings of Yorkshire, amaze and bewilder foreigners, who perhaps imagine that they do not understand English, when they are in company with those who cannot speak it. The patois of Languedoc and Champagne,[184] such as '*Mien fis sest ai bai via*,' Mon fils c'est un beau veau, exercises, it is true, the ingenuity of travellers, and renders many scenes of Moliere and Marivaux[185] difficult, if not unintelligible, to those who have never resided in the French provinces; but no French patois is more unintelligible than the following specimen of *Tummas* and *Meary*'s Lancashire dialogue: –

Thomas. 'Whau, but I startit up to goa to th' tits, on slurr'd deawn to th' lower part o' th' heymough, on by th' maskins, lord! whot dusk think? boh leet hump stridd'n up o' summot ot felt meety heury, on it startit weh meh on its back, deawn th' lower part o' th'mough it jumpt, crost th' leath, eaw't o' th' dur whimmey it took, on into th' weturing poo, os if th' dule o' hell had driv'n it, on there it threw meh en, or I fell off, I connaw tell whether, for th' life o' meh, into the poo.'

Mary. 'Whoo-wo, whoo-wo, whoo! whot, ith neme o' God! widneh sey?'

Thomas. 'If it wur naw Owd Nick, he wur th' orderer on't, to be shure. Weh mitch powlering I geet eawt o' th' poo, 'lieve* meh, as to list, I could na tell whether i'r in a sleawm or wak'n, till eh groapt ot meh een; I crope under a wough and stode like o' gawmbling†, or o parfit neatril, till welly day,' &c.[186]

Let us now listen to a conversation which we hope will not be quite so unintelligible.

---

* The glossary to the Lancashire dialect informs us, that *'lieve me* comes from *beleemy*, believe me; from *belamy*, my good friend, *old French*.
† Gawmbling (*Anglo Saxon* gawmless), stupid.

Chapter XII

Bath Coach Conversation

In one of the coaches which travel between Bath and London, an Irish, a Scotch, and an English gentleman happened to be passengers. They were well informed and well-bred, had seen the world, had lived in good company, and were consequently superior to local and national prejudice. As their conversation was illustrative of our subject, we shall make no apology for relating it. We pass the usual preliminary compliments, and the observations upon the weather and the roads. The Irish gentleman first started a more interesting subject – the Union; its probable advantages and disadvantages were fully discussed, and, at last, the Irishman said, 'Whatever our political opinions may be, there is one wish in which we shall all agree, that the Union may make us better acquainted with one another.'

'It is surprising,' said the Englishman, 'how ignorant we English in general are of Ireland: to be sure we do not now, as in the times of Bacon and Spenser, believe that wild Irishmen have wings;[187] nor do we all of us give credit to Mr Twiss's assertion, that if you look at an Irish lady, she answers, "*port, if you please.*"'[188]

Scotchman. – 'That traveller seems to be almost as liberal as he who defined *oats* – food for horses in England, and for men in Scotland:[189] such illiberal notions die away of themselves.'

Irishman. – 'Or they are contradicted by more liberal travellers. I am sure my country has great obligations to the gallant English and Scotch military, not only for so readily assisting to defend and quiet us, but for spreading in England a juster notion of Ireland. Within these few months, I suppose, more real knowledge of the state and manners of that kingdom has been diffused in England by their means, than had been obtained during a whole century.'

Scotchman. – 'Indeed, I do not recollect having read any author of note who has given me a notion of Ireland since Spenser and Davies, except Arthur Young.'[190]

Englishman. – 'What little knowledge I have of Ireland has been drawn more from observation than from books. I remember when I first went over there, I did not expect to see twenty trees in the whole island: I imagined that I should have nothing to drink but whiskey, that I should have nothing to eat but potatoes, that I should sleep in mud-walled cabins; that I should, when awake, hear nothing but the Irish howl, the Irish brogue, Irish answers, and

Irish bulls; and that if I smiled at any of these things, a hundred pistols would fly from their holsters[191] to *give* or *demand* satisfaction. But experience taught me better things: I found that the stories I had heard were *tales of other times*. Their hospitality, indeed, continues to this day.

Irishman. – 'It does, I believe; but of later days, as we have been honoured with the visits of a greater number of foreigners, our hospitality has become less extravagant.'

Englishman. – 'Not less agreeable: Irish hospitality, I speak from experience, does not now consist merely in pushing about the bottle; the Irish are convivial, but their conviviality is seasoned with wit and humour; they have plenty of good conversation as well as good cheer for their guests; and they not only have wit themselves, but they love it in others: they can take as well as give a joke. I never lived with a more good-humoured, generous, open-hearted people than the Irish.'

Irishman. – 'I wish Englishmen, in general, were half as partial to poor Ireland as you are, sir.'

Englishman. – 'Or rather you wish that they knew the country as well, and then they would do it as much justice.'

Irishman. – 'You do it something more than justice, I fear. There are little peculiarities in my countrymen which will long be justly the subject of ridicule in England.'

Scotchman. – 'Not among well-bred and well-informed people: those who have seen or read of great varieties of customs and manners are never apt to laugh at all that may differ from their own. As the sensible author of the Government of the Tongue says, "Half-witted people are always the bitterest revilers."'[192]

Irishman. – 'You are very indulgent, gentlemen; but, in spite of all your politeness, you must allow, or, at least, I must confess, that there are little defects in the Irish government of the tongue at which even *whole*-witted people must laugh.'

Scotchman. – 'The well-educated people in all countries, I believe, escape the particular accent, and avoid the idiom, that are characteristic of the vulgar.'

Irishman. – 'But even when we escape Irish brogue we cannot escape Irish bulls.'

Englishman. – 'You need not say *Irish* bulls with such emphasis; for bulls are not peculiar to Ireland. I have been informed by a person of unquestionable authority, that there is a town in Germany, Hirschau in the Upper Palatinate, where the inhabitants are famous for making bulls.'[193]

Irishman. – 'I am truly glad to hear we have companions in disgrace. Numbers certainly lessen the effect of ridicule as well as of shame: but, after all, the Irish idiom is peculiarly unfortunate, for it leads perpetually to blunder.'

Scotchman. – 'I have heard the same remarked of the Hebrew. I am told that the Hebrew and Irish idiom are much alike.'

Irishman (laughing). – 'That is a great comfort to us, certainly, particularly to those amongst us who are fond of tracing our origin up to the remotest antiquity; but still there are many who would willingly give up the honour of this high alliance to avoid its inconveniences; for my own part, if I could ensure myself and my countrymen from all future danger of making bulls and blunders, I would this instant give up all Hebrew roots; and even the Ogham[194] character itself I would renounce, "to make assurance doubly sure."'[195]

Englishman. – '"To make *assurance doubly sure.*" Now there is an example in our great Shakspeare of what I have often observed, that we English allow our poets and ourselves a license of speech that we deny to our Hibernian neighbours. If an Irishman, instead of Shakspeare, had talked of making "assurance doubly sure," we should have asked how that could be. The vulgar in England are too apt to catch at every slip of the tongue made by Irishmen. I remember once being present when an Irish nobleman, of talents and literature, was actually hissed from the hustings at a Middlesex election because in his speech he happened to say, "We have laid the root to the axe of the tree of liberty," instead of "we have laid the axe to the root of the tree."'

Scotchman. – 'A lapsus linguæ, that might have been made by the greatest orators, ancient or modern; by Cicero or Chatham, by Burke, or by "the fluent Murray."'[196]

Englishman. – 'Upon another occasion I have heard that an Irish orator was silenced with "*inextinguishable* laughter" merely for saying, "I am sorry to hear my honourable friend stand mute."'

Scotchman. – 'If I am not mistaken, that very same Irish orator made an allusion at which no one could laugh. "The protection," said he, "which Britain affords to Ireland in the day of adversity, is like that which the oak affords to the ignorant countryman, who flies to it for shelter in the storm; it draws down upon his head the lightning of heaven:" may be I do not repeat the words exactly, but I could not forget the idea.'

Englishman. – 'I would with all my heart bear the ridicule of a hundred blunders for the honour of having made such a simile: after all, his saying, "I am sorry to hear my honourable friend stand *mute*," if it be a bull, is justified by Homer; one of the charms in the cestus of Venus is,

"*Silence* that *speaks*, and eloquence of eyes."' [197]

Scotchman. – '*Silence that speaks*, sir, is, I am afraid, an English, not a Grecian charm. It is not in the Greek; it is one of those beautiful liberties which Mr Pope has taken with his original. But silence that speaks can be found in France as well as in England. Voltaire, in his chef-d'œuvre, his Œdipus, makes Jocasta say,

"Tout *parle* contre nous jusqu'a notre *silence*."'*¹⁹⁸

Englishman. – 'And in our own Milton, Samson Agonistes makes as good, indeed a better, bull; for he not only makes the mute speak, but speak loud: –

"The deeds themselves, though *mute, spoke loud* the doer."¹⁹⁹

And in Paradise Lost we have, to speak in *fashionable* language, two *famous* bulls. Talking of Satan, Milton says,

"God and his Son except,
Created thing nought valued he nor shunn'd."²⁰⁰

And speaking of Adam and Eve, and their sons and daughters, he confounds them all together in a manner for which any Irishman would have been laughed to scorn: –

"Adam, the goodliest man of men since born,
His sons; the fairest of her daughters Eve."²⁰¹

Yet Addison, who notices these blunders, calls them only little blemishes.'²⁰²

Scotchman. – 'He does so; and he quotes Horace, who tells us we should impute such venial errors to a pardonable inadvertency; and, as I recollect, Addison makes another very just remark, that the ancients, who were actuated by a spirit of candour, not of cavilling, invented a variety of figures of speech, on purpose to palliate little errors of this nature.'²⁰³

'Really, gentlemen,' interrupted the Hibernian, who had sat all this time in silence that *spoke* his grateful sense of the politeness of

---

* 'Every thing speaks against us, even our silence.'

his companions, 'you will put the finishing stroke to my obligations to you, if you will prove that the ancient figures of speech were invented to palliate Irish blunders.'

Englishman. – 'No matter for what purpose they were invented; if we can make so good a use of them we shall be satisfied, especially if you are pleased. I will, however, leave the burthen of the proof upon my friend here, who has detected me already in quoting from Pope's Iliad instead of Homer's. I am sure he will manage the ancient figures of rhetoric better than I should; however, if I can fight behind his shield I shall not shun the combat.'

Scotchman. – 'I stand corrected for quoting Greek. Now I will not go to Longinus for my tropes and figures; I have just met with a little book on the subject, which I put into my pocket today, intending to finish it on my journey, but I have been better employed.'

He drew from his pocket a book, called 'Deinology; or the Union of Reason and Elegance.'[204] 'Look,' said he, 'look at this long list of tropes and figures; amongst them we could find apologies for every species of Irish bulls; but, in mercy, I will select, from "the twenty chief and most moving figures of speech," only the oxymoron, as it is a favourite with Irish orators. In the oxymoron contradictions meet: to reconcile these, Irish ingenuity delights. I will further spare four out of the seven figures of less note: emphasis, enallage, and the hysteron proteron you must have; because emphasis graces Irish diction, enallage unbinds it from strict grammatical letters, and hysteron proteron allows it sometimes to put the cart before the horse. Of the eleven grammatical figures, Ireland delights chiefly in the antimeria, or changing one part of speech for another, and in the ellipsis or defect. Of the remaining long list of figures, the Irish are particularly disposed to the epizeuxis, as "indeed, indeed – at all, at all," and antanaclasis, or double meaning. The tautotes, or repetition of the same thing, is, I think, full as common amongst the English. The hyperbole and catachresis are so nearly related to a bull, that I shall dwell upon them with pleasure. You must listen to the definition of a catachresis: – "A catachresis is the boldest of any trope. *Necessity makes it borrow and employ an expression or term contrary to the thing it means to express.*"'[205]

'Upon my word this is something like a description of an Irish bull,' interrupted the Hibernian.

Scotchman. – 'For instance, it has been said, *Equitare in arundine longâ*, to ride on horseback on a stick.[206] Reason condemns the contradiction, but necessity has allowed it, and use has made it intelligible. The same trope is employed in the following metaphorical expression: – the seeds of the Gospel have been *watered* with the *blood* of the martyrs.'[207]

Englishman. – 'That does seem an absurdity', I grant; but you know great orators *trample on impossibilities.*'*

Scotchman. – 'And great poets *get the better of them.* You recollect Shakspeare says,

> "Now bid me run,
> And I will strive with things *impossible*,
> Yea, *get the better of them.*"' [208]

Englishman. – 'And Corneille, in the Cid, I believe, makes his hero a compliment upon his having performed impossibilities – "Vos mains seules ont le droit de vaincre un invincible."'[209]†

Scotchman. – 'Ay, that would be a bull in an Irishman, but it is only an hyperbole in a Frenchman.'

Irishman. – 'Indeed this line of Corneille's *out hyperboles* the hyperbole, considered in any but a prophetic light; as a prophecy, it

---

* Lord Chatham.[210]
† Your hands alone have a right to conquer *the unconquerable.*

exactly foretels the taking of Bonaparte's *invincible* standard by the glorious forty-second regiment of the British:[211] "Your hands alone *have a right* to vanquish the invincible." By the by, the phrase *ont le droit* cannot, I believe, be literally translated into English; but the Scotch and Irish, *have a right*, translates it exactly. But do not let me interrupt my country's defence, gentlemen; I am heartily glad to find Irish blunderers may shelter themselves in such good company in the ancient sanctuary of the hyperbole. But I am afraid you must deny admittance to the poor mason, who said, "this house will stand as long as the world, and longer."'

Scotchman. – 'Why should we "shut the gates of mercy"[212] upon him, when we pardon his betters for more flagrant sins; for instance, Mr Pope, who, in his Essay on Criticism, makes a blunder, or rather uses an hyperbole, stronger than that of your poor Irish mason: –

"When first young Maro in his noble mind
A work *t'outlast immortal* Rome design'd." [213]

And to give you a more modern case, I lately heard an English shopkeeper say to a lady in recommendation of his goods, "Ma'am, it will wear for ever, and make you a petticoat afterwards."'

Irishman. – 'Upon my word, I did not think you could have found a match for the mason; but what will you say to my countryman, who, on meeting an acquaintance, accosted him with this ambiguous compliment – "When first I saw you I thought it was you, but now I see it is your brother."'

Scotchman. – 'If I were not afraid you would take me for a pedant, I should quote a sentence from Cicero that is not far behind this blunder.'

Irishman. – 'I can take you for nothing but a friend: pray let us have the Latin.'

Scotchman. – 'It is one of Cicero's compliments to Cæsar – "Qui, cum ipse imperator in toto imperio populi Romani unus esset, esse me alterum passus est."'[214]* 'Perhaps,' continued the Scotchman, 'my way of pronouncing Latin sounds strangely to you, gentlemen?'

Irishman. – 'And perhaps ours would be unintelligible to Cicero himself, if he were to overhear us: I fancy we are all so far from right, that we need not dispute about degrees of wrong.'

The coach stopped at this instant, and the conversation was interrupted.

* And when Cæsar was the *only emperor* within the dominion of Rome, he suffered me to be *another*.

Chapter XIII

Bath Coach Conversation

After our travellers had dined, the conversation was renewed by the English gentleman's repeating Goldsmith's celebrated lines on Burke:

> 'Who, too deep for his hearers, still went on refining,
> And thought of convincing, whilst they thought of dining;
> In short, 'twas his fate, unemploy'd or in place, sir,
> To eat mutton cold, and cut blocks with a razor.'[215]

'What humour and wit there are in that poem of Goldsmith's! and where is there any thing equal to his "Traveller?"'[216]

Irishman. – 'Yet this is the man who used to be the butt of the company for his bulls.'

Englishman. – 'No, not for his bulls, but for *blurting* out opinions in conversation that could not stand the test of Dr Johnson's critical powers. But what would become of the freedom of wit and humour if every word that came out of our mouths were subject to the tax of a professed critic's censure, or if every sentence were to undergo a logical examination? It would be well for Englishmen if they were a little more inclined, like your open-hearted countrymen, to *blurt* out their opinions freely.'

Scotchman. – 'I cannot forgive Dr Johnson for calling Goldsmith an inspired idiot; I confess I see no idiotism, but much inspiration, in his works.'

Irishman. – 'But we must remember, that if Johnson did laugh at Goldsmith, he would let no one else laugh at him, and he was his most sincere and active friend. The world would, perhaps, never have seen the "Vicar of Wakefield" if Johnson had not recommended it to a bookseller; and Goldsmith might have died in gaol if the doctor had not got him a hundred pounds for it, when poor Goldsmith did not know it was worth a shilling.[217] When we recollect this, we must forgive the doctor for calling him, in jest, an inspired idiot.'

Scotchman. – 'Especially as Goldsmith has wit enough to bear him up against a thousand such jests.'

Englishman. – 'It is curious to observe how nearly wit and absurdity are allied. We may forgive the genius of Ireland if he sometimes

"Leap his light courser o'er the bounds of taste."[218]

Even English genius is not always to be restrained within the strict limits of common sense. For instance, Young is witty when he says

> "How would a miser startle to be told
> Of such a wonder as insolvent gold." [219]

But Johnson is, I am afraid, absurd when he says,

> "Turn from the glittering bribe your scornful eye,
> Nor sell for gold what gold can never buy.'" [220]

'One case, to be sure, must be excepted,' said the Irishman; 'a patriot may sell his reputation, and the purchaser get nothing by it. But, gentlemen, I have just recollected an example of an Irish bull in which are all the happy requisites, incongruity, confusion, and laughable confusion, both in thought and expression. When sir Richard Steele was asked, how it happened that his countrymen made so many bulls, he replied, "It is the effect of climate, sir; if an Englishman were born in Ireland, he would make as many."' [221]

Scotchman. – 'This is an excellent bull, I allow; but I think I can match it.'

Englishman. – 'And if he can, you will allow yourself to be fairly vanquished?'

Irishman. – 'Most *willingly*.'

Scotchman. – 'Then I shall owe my victory to our friend Dr Johnson, the leviathan of English literature. In his celebrated preface to Shakspeare he says, that "he has not only shown human nature as it acts in real exigences, but as it *would be found in situations to which it cannot be exposed.*" [222] These are his own words, I think I remember them accurately.'

The English gentleman smiled, and our Hibernian acknowledged that the Scotchman had fairly gained the victory. 'My friends,' added he, 'as I cannot pretend to be "convinced against my will," I certainly am not "of the same opinion still." But stay – there are such things as practical bulls: did you never hear of the Irishman who ordered a painter to draw his picture, and to represent him standing behind a tree?'

Englishman. – 'No: but I have heard the very same story told of an Englishman. The dealers in *good jokes* give them first to one nation and then to another, first to one celebrated character and then to another, as it suits the demand and fashion of the day: just as our printsellers, with a few touches, change the portrait of general Washington into the head of the king of France, and a capital print of sir Joshua Reynolds into a striking likeness of *the Monster*.[223]

'But I can give you an instance of a practical bull that is not only indisputably English, but was made by one of the greatest men that England ever produced, sir Isaac Newton, who, after he had made a large hole in his study-door for his cat to creep through, made a small hole beside it for the kitten.[224] You will acknowledge, sir, that this is a good practical bull.'

'Pardon me,' said the Hibernian, 'we have still some miles further to go, and, if you will give me leave, I will relate "an Hibernian tale," which exemplifies some of the opinions held in this conversation.'

The Scotch and English gentlemen begged to hear the story, and he began in the following manner.

Chapter XIV

The Irish Incognito

Sir John Bull was a native of Ireland, *bred* and *born* in the city of Cork. His real name was Phelim O'Mooney, and he was by profession a *stocah*, or walking gentleman; that is, a person who is too proud to earn his bread, and too poor to have bread without earning it. He had always been told that none of his ancestors had ever been in trade or business of any kind, and he resolved, when a boy, never to *demean* himself and family, as his elder brother had done, by becoming a rich merchant. When he grew up to be a young man he kept this spirited resolution as long as he had a relation or friend in the world who would let him hang upon them; but when he was shaken off by all, what could he do but go into business? He chose the most genteel, however; he became a wine merchant. I'm *only* a wine merchant, said he to himself, and that is next door to being nothing at all. His brother furnished his cellars; and Mr Phelim O'Mooney, upon the strength of the wine that he had in his cellars, and of the money he expected to make of it, immediately married a wife, set up a gig, and gave excellent dinners to men who were ten times richer than he even ever *expected* to be. In return for these excellent dinners, his new friends bought all their wine from Mr O'Mooney, and never paid for it; he lived upon credit himself, and gave all his friends credit, till he became a bankrupt. Then nobody came to dine with him, and every body found out that he had been very imprudent; and he was obliged to sell his gig, but not before it had broken his wife's neck; so that when accounts came to be finally settled, he was not much worse than when he began the world, the loss falling upon his creditors, and he being, as he observed, free to begin life again, with the advantage of being once more a bachelor. He was such a good-natured, free-hearted fellow, that every body liked him, even his creditors. His wife's relations made up the sum of five hundred pounds for him, and his brother offered to take him into his firm as partner; but O'Mooney preferred, he said, going to try, or rather to make, his fortune in England, as he did not doubt but he should by marriage, being, as he did not scruple to acknowledge, a personable, clever-looking man, and a great favourite with the sex.

'My last wife I married for love, my next I expect will do the same by me, and of course the money must come on her side this time,' said our hero, half jesting, half in earnest. His elder and wiser brother, the merchant, whom he still held in more than sufficient contempt, ventured to hint some slight objections to this scheme of Phelim's seeking fortune in England. He observed that so many had gone upon this plan already, that there was rather a prejudice in England against Irish adventurers.

This could not affect *him* any ways, Phelim replied, because he did not mean to appear in England as an Irishman at all.

'How then?'

'As an Englishman, since that is most agreeable.'

'How can that be?'

'Who should hinder it?'

His brother, hesitatingly, said, 'Yourself.'

'Myself! – What part of myself? Is it my tongue? – You'll acknowledge, brother, that I do not speak with the brogue.'

It was true that Phelim did not speak with any Irish brogue; his mother was an English woman, and he had lived much with English officers in Cork, and he had studied and imitated their manner of speaking so successfully, that no one, merely by his accent, could have guessed that he was an Irishman.

'Hey! brother, I say!' continued Phelim, in a triumphant English tone; 'I never was taken for an Irishman in my life. Colonel Broadman told me, the other day, I spoke English better than the English themselves; that he should take me for an Englishman, in any part of the known world, the moment I opened my lips. You must allow that not the smallest particle of brogue is discernible on my tongue.'

His brother allowed that not the smallest particle of brogue was to be discerned upon Phelim's tongue, but feared that some Irish idiom might be perceived in his conversation. And then the name of O'Mooney!

'O, as to that, I need not trouble an act of parliament, or even a king's letter, just to change my name for a season; at the worst, I can travel and appear incognito.'

'Always?'

'No: only just till I'm upon good terms with the lady — Mrs Phelim O'Mooney, that is to be, God willing. Never fear, nor shake your head, brother; *you* men of business are out of this line, and not proper judges: I beg your pardon for saying so, but as you are my own brother, and nobody by, you'll excuse me.'

His brother did excuse him, but continued silent for some minutes; he was pondering upon the means of persuading Phelim to give up this scheme.

'I would lay you any wager, my dear Phelim,' said he, 'that you could not continue four days in England incognito.'

'Done!' cried Phelim. 'Done for a hundred pounds; done for a thousand pounds, and welcome.'

'But if you lose, how will you pay?'

'Faith! that's the last thing I thought of, being sure of winning.'

'Then you will not object to any mode of payment I shall propose.'

'None: only remembering always, that I was a bankrupt last week, and shall be little better till I'm married; but then I'll pay you honestly, if I lose.'

'No, if you lose I must be paid before that time, my good sir,' said his brother, laughing. 'My bet is this: – I will lay you one hundred guineas that you do not remain four days in England incognito; be upon honour with me, and promise, that if you lose you will, instead of laying down a hundred guineas, come back immediately, and settle quietly again to business.'

The word *business* was always odious to our hero's proud ears; but he thought himself so secure of winning his wager, that he willingly bound himself in a penalty which he believed would never become due; and his generous brother, at parting, made the bet still more favourable, by allowing that Phelim should not be deemed the loser unless he was, in the course of the first four days after he touched English ground, detected eight times in being an Irishman.

'Eight times!' cried Phelim. 'Good bye to a hundred guineas, brother, you may say.'

'You may say,' echoed his brother, and so they parted.

Mr Phelim O'Mooney the next morning sailed from Cork harbour with a prosperous gale, and with a confidence in his own success which supplied the place of auspicious omens. He embarked at Cork, to go by long sea to London, and was driven into Deal, where Julius Cæsar once landed before him, and with the same resolution to see and conquer.[225] It was early in the morning; having been very sea-sick, he was impatient, as soon as he got into the inn, for his breakfast: he was shown into a room where three ladies were waiting to go by the stage; his air of easy confidence was the best possible introduction.

'Would any of the company choose eggs?' said the waiter.

'I never touch an egg for my share,' said O'Mooney, carelessly; he knew that it was supposed to be an Irish custom to eat eggs at breakfast; and when the malicious waiter afterward set a plate full of eggs in salt upon the table, our hero magnanimously abstained from them; he even laughed heartily at a story told by one of the ladies of an Hibernian at Buxton, who declared that 'no English hen ever laid a fresh egg.'

O'Mooney got through breakfast much to his own satisfaction, and to that of the ladies, whom he had taken a proper occasion to call the *three graces*, and whom he had informed that he was an *old* baronet of an English family, and that his name was sir John Bull. The youngest of the graces civilly observed, 'that whatever else he might be, she should never have taken him for an *old* baronet.' The lady who made this speech was pretty, but O'Mooney had penetration enough to discover, in the course of the conversation, that she and her companions were far from being divinities: his three graces were a greengrocer's wife, a tallowchandler's widow, and a milliner. When he found that these ladies were likely to be his companions if he were to travel in the coach, he changed his plan, and ordered a postchaise and four.

O'Mooney was not in danger of making any vulgar Irish blunders in paying his bill at an inn. No landlord or waiter could have suspected him, especially as he always left them to settle the matter first, and then looked over the bill and money with a careless gentility, saying, 'Very right,' or, 'Very well, sir;' wisely calculating, that it was better to lose a few shillings on the road than to lose a hundred pounds by the risk of Hibernian miscalculation.

Whilst the chaise was getting ready, he went to the customhouse to look after his baggage. He found a red-hot countryman of his own there, roaring about four and fourpence, and fighting the battle of his trunks, in which he was ready to make affidavit there was not, nor never had been, any thing contraband; and when the custom-house officer replied by pulling out of one of them a piece of Irish poplin, the Hibernian fell immediately upon the Union, which he swore was Disunion, as the custom-house officers managed it. Sir John Bull appeared to much advantage all this time, maintaining a dignified silence; from his quiet appearance and deportment, the custom-house officers took it for granted that he was an Englishman. He was in no hurry; he begged *that* gentleman's business might be settled first; he would wait the officer's leisure, and as he spoke he played so dexterously with half-a-guinea between his fingers as to make it visible only where he wished. The custom-house officer was his humble servant immediately; but the Hibernian would have been his enemy, if he had not conciliated him by observing, 'that even Englishmen must allow there was something very like a bull in professing to make a complete identification of the two kingdoms, whilst, at the same time, certain regulations continued in full force to divide the countries by art, even more than the British channel does by nature.'

Sir John talked so plausibly, and, above all, so candidly and coolly on Irish and English politics, that the custom-house officer conversed with him for a quarter of an hour without guessing of what country he was, till in an unlucky moment Phelim's heart got the better of his head. Joining in the praises bestowed by all parties on the conduct of a distinguished patriot of his country, he, in the height of his enthusiasm, inadvertently called him *the Speaker*.[226]

'The *Speaker*!' said the officer.

'Yes, the Speaker – *our* Speaker!' cried Phelim, with exultation. He was not aware how he had betrayed himself, till the officer smiled and said –

'Sir, I really never should have found out that you were an Irishman but from the manner in which you named your countryman, who is as highly thought of by all parties in this country as in yours: your enthusiasm does honour to your heart.'

'And to my head, I'm sure,' said our hero, laughing with the best grace imaginable. 'Well! I am glad you have found me out in this manner, though I lose the eighth part of a bet of a hundred guineas by it.'

He explained the wager, and begged the custom-house officer to keep his secret, which he promised to do faithfully, and assured him, that 'he should be happy to do any thing in his power to serve him.' Whilst he was uttering these last words, there came in a snug, but soft-looking Englishman, who opining from the words 'happy to do any thing in my power to serve you' that O'Mooney was a friend of the custom-house officer's, and encouraged by something affable and good-natured in our hero's countenance, crept up to him, and whispered a request – 'Could you tell a body, sir, how to get out of the custom-house a very valuable box of Sèvre china that has been *laying* in the custom-house three weeks, and which I was commissioned to get out if I could, and bring up to town for a lady.'

As a lady was in the case, O'Mooney's gallantry instantly made his good-nature effective. The box of Sèvre china was produced, and opened only as a matter of form, and only as a matter of curiosity its contents were examined – a beautiful set of Sèvre china and a pendule, said to have belonged to M. Egalité![227] 'These things must be intended,' said Phelim, 'for some lady of superior taste or fortune.'

As Phelim was a proficient in the Socratic art of putting judicious interrogatories, he was soon happily master of the principal points it concerned him to know: he learnt that the lady was rich – a spinster – of full age – at her own disposal – living with a single female companion at Blackheath[228] – furnishing a house there in a superior style – had two carriages – her Christian name Mary – her surname Sharperson.

O'Mooney, by the blessing of God, it shall soon be, thought Phelim. He politely offered the Englishman a place in his chaise for himself and Sèvre china, as it was for a lady, and would run great hazard in the stage, which besides was full. Mr Queasy, for that was our soft Englishman's name, was astonished by our hero's condescension and affability, especially as he heard him called sir John: he bowed sundry times as low as the fear of losing his wig would permit, and accepted the polite offer with many thanks for himself and the lady concerned.

Sir John Bull's chaise and four was soon ready; and Queasy seated in the corner of it, and the Sèvre china safely stowed between his knees. Captain Murray, a Scotch officer, was standing at the inn door, with his eyes intently fixed on the letters that were worked in nails on the top of sir John's trunk; the letters were P. O'M. Our hero, whose eyes were at least as quick as the Scotchman's, was alarmed lest this should lead to a second detection. He called instantly, with his usual presence of mind, to the ostler, and desired him to uncord *that* trunk, as it was not to go with him; raising his voice loud enough for all *the yard* to hear, he added – 'It is not mine at all; it belongs to my friend Mr O'Mooney: let it be sent after me, at leisure, by the waggon, as directed, to the care of sir John Bull.'

Our hero was now giving his invention a prodigious quantity of superfluous trouble; and upon this occasion, as upon most others, he was more in danger from excess than deficiency of ingenuity: he was like the man in the fairy tale, who was obliged to tie his legs lest he should outrun the object of which he was in pursuit.[229] The Scotch officer, though his eyes were fixed on the letters P. O'M., had none of the suspicions which Phelim was counteracting; he was only considering how he could ask for the third place in sir John's chaise during the next stage, as he was in great haste to get to town upon particular business, and there were no other horses at the inn. When he heard that the heavy baggage was to go by waggon, he took courage, and made his request. It was instantly granted by the good-natured Hibernian, who showed as much hospitality about his chaise as if it had been his house. Away they drove as fast as they could. Fresh dangers awaited him at the next inn. He left his hat upon the table in the hall whilst he went into the parlour, and when he returned, he heard some person' inquiring what Irish gentleman was there. Our hero was terribly alarmed, for he saw that his hat was in the inquirer's hand, and he recollected that the name of Phelim O'Mooney was written in it. This the inquisitive gentleman did not see, for it was written in no very legible characters on the leather withinside of the front; but 'F. Guest, hatter, Dame-street, Dublin,' was a printed advertisement that could not be mistaken, and *that* was pasted within the crown. O'Mooney's presence of mind did not forsake him upon this emergency.

'My good sir,' said he, turning to Queasy, who, without hearing one word of what was passing, was coming out of the parlour with his own hat and gloves in his hand; 'My good sir,' continued he, loading him with parcels, 'will you have the goodness to see these put into my carriage? I'll take care of your hat and gloves,' added O'Mooney in a low voice. Queasy surrendered his hat and gloves instantly, unknowing wherefore; then squeezed forward with his load through the crowd, crying – 'Waiter! hostler! pray, somebody put these into sir John Bull's chaise.'

Sir John Bull, equipped, with Queasy's hat, marched deliberately through the defile, bowing with the air of at least an English county member[230] to this side and to that, as way was made for him to his carriage. No one suspected that the hat did not belong to him; no one, indeed, thought of the hat, for all eyes were fixed upon the man. Seated in the carriage, he threw money to the waiter, hostler, and boots, and drew up the glass, bidding the postilions drive on. By this cool self-possession our hero effected his retreat with successful generalship, leaving his new Dublin beaver behind him, without regret, as bona waviata.[231] Queasy, before whose eyes things passed continually without his seeing them, thanked sir John for the care he had taken of his hat, drew on his gloves, and calculated aloud how long they should be going to the next stage. At the first town they passed through, O'Mooney bought a new hat, and Queasy deplored the unaccountable mistake by which sir John's hat had been forgotten. No further *mistakes* happened upon the journey. The travellers rattled on, and neither 'stinted nor stayed'[232] till they arrived at Blackheath, at miss Sharperson's. Sir John sat Queasy down without having given him the least hint of his designs upon the lady; but as he helped him out with the Sèvre china, he looked through the large opening double doors of the hall, and slightly said – 'Upon my word, this seems to be a handsome house: it would be worth looking at, if the family were not at home.'

'I am morally sure, sir John,' said the soft Queasy, 'that miss Sharperson would be happy to let you see the house to-night, and this minute, if she knew you were at the door, and who you were, and all your civility about me and the china. – Do, pray, walk in.'

'Not for the world: a gentleman could not do such a thing without an invitation from the lady of the house herself.'

'Oh, if that's all, I'll step up myself to the young lady; I'm certain she'll be proud —'

'Mr Queasy, by no means; I would not have the lady disturbed for the world at this unseasonable hour. – It is too late – quite too late.'

'Not at all, begging pardon, sir John,' said Queasy, taking out his watch: 'only just tea-time by me. – Not at all unseasonable for any body; besides, the message is of my own head: – all, you know, if not well taken —'

Up the great staircase he made bold to go on his mission, as he thought, in defiance of sir John's better judgment. He returned in a few minutes with a face of self-complacent exultation *and* miss Sharperson's compliments, and begs sir John Bull will walk up and rest himself with a dish of tea, and has her thanks to him for the china.

Now Queasy, who had the highest possible opinion of sir John Bull and of miss Sharperson, whom he thought the two people of the greatest consequence and affability, had formed the notion that they were made for each other, and that it must be a match if they could but meet. The meeting he had now happily contrived and effected; and he had done his part for his friend sir John, with miss Sharperson, by as many exaggerations as he could utter in five minutes, concerning his perdigious politeness and courage, his fine person and carriage, his ancient family, and vast connections and importance wherever he appeared on the road, at inns, and over all England. He had previously, during the journey, done his part for his friend miss Sharperson with sir John, by stating that 'she had a large fortune left her by her mother, and was to have twice as much from her grandmother; that she had thousands upon thousands in the funds, and an estate of two thousand a year, called Rascàlly, in Scotland, besides plate and jewels without end.'

Thus prepared, how could this lady and gentleman meet without falling desperately in love with each other!

Though a servant in handsome livery appeared ready to show sir John up the great staircase, Mr Queasy acted as a gentleman usher, or rather as showman. He nodded to sir John as they passed across a long gallery and through an ante-chamber, threw open the doors of various apartments as he went along, crying – 'Peep in! peep in! peep in here! peep in there! – Is not this spacious? Is not this elegant? Is not that grand? Did I say too much?' continued he, rubbing his hands with delight. 'Did you ever see so magnificent and such highly-polished steel grates out of Lon'on?'

Sir John, conscious that the servant's eyes were upon him, smiled at this question, 'looked superior down;'[233] and though with reluctant complaisance he leaned his body to this side or to that, as Queasy pulled or swayed, yet he appeared totally regardless of the man's vulgar reflections. He had seen every thing as he passed, and was surprised at all he saw; but he evinced not the slightest symptom of astonishment. He was now ushered into a spacious, well-lighted apartment: he entered with the easy, unembarrassed air of a man who was perfectly accustomed to such a home. His quick coup-d'œil took in the whole at a single glance. Two magnificent candelabras stood on Egyptian tables at the farther end of the room, and the lights were reflected on all sides from mirrors of no common size. Nothing seemed worthy to attract our hero's attention but the lady of the house, whom he approached with an air of distinguished respect. She was reclining on a Turkish sofa, her companion seated beside her, tuning a harp. Miss Sharperson half rose to receive sir John: he paid his compliments with an easy, yet respectful air. He was thanked for his civilities to *the person* who had been commissioned to bring the box of Sèvre china from Deal.

'Vastly sorry it should have been so troublesome,' miss Sharperson said, in a voice fashionably unintelligible, and with a most becoming yet intimidating nonchalance of manner. Intimidating it might have been to any man but our hero; he, who had the happy talent of catching, wherever he went, the reigning manner of the place, replied to the lady in equal strains; and she, in her turn, seemed to look upon him more as her equal. Tea and coffee were served. *Nothings* were talked of quite easily by sir John. He practised the art 'not to admire,'[234] so as to give a justly high opinion of his taste, consequence, and knowledge of the world. Miss Sharperson, though her nonchalance was much diminished, continued to maintain a certain dignified reserve; whilst her companion, miss Felicia Flat,[235] condescended to ask sir John, who had doubtless seen every fine house in England and on the continent, his opinion with respect to the furniture and finishing of the room, the placing of the Egyptian tables and the candelabras.

No mortal could have guessed by sir John Bull's air, when he heard this question, that he had never seen a candelabra before in his life. He was so much, and yet seemingly so little upon his guard, he dealt so dexterously in generals, and evaded particulars so delicately, that he went through this dangerous conversation triumphantly. Careful not to protract his visit beyond the bounds of propriety, he soon rose to take leave, and he mingled 'intrusion, regret, late hour, happiness, and honour,'[236] so charmingly in his parting compliment, as to leave the most favourable impression on the minds of both ladies, and to procure for himself an invitation to see the house next morning.

The first day was now ended, and our hero had been detected but once. He went to rest this night well satisfied with himself, but much more occupied with the hopes of marrying the heiress of Rascàlly than of winning a paltry bet.

The next day he waited upon the ladies in high spirits. Neither of them was *visible*, but Mr Queasy had orders to show him the house, which he did with much exultation, dwelling particularly in his praises on the beautiful high polish of the steel grates. Queasy boasted that it was he who had recommended the ironmonger who furnished the house in that line; and that his bill, as he was proud to state, amounted to *many*, *many* hundreds. Sir John, who did not attend to one word Queasy said, went to examine the map of the Rascàlly estate, which was unrolled, and he had leisure to count the number of lords' and ladies' visiting tickets which lay upon the chimney-piece. He saw names of people of the first quality and respectability: it was plain that Miss Sharperson must be a lady of high family as well as large fortune, else she would not be visited by persons of such distinction. Our hero's passion for her increased every moment. Her companion, miss Flat, now appeared, and entered very freely into conversation with sir John; and as he perceived that she was commissioned to sit in judgment upon him, he evaded all her leading questions with the skill of an Irish witness, but without giving any Hibernian answers. She was fairly at a fault.[237] Miss Sharperson at length appeared, elegantly dressed; her person was genteel, and her face rather pretty. Sir John, at this instant, thought her beautiful, or seemed to think so. The ladies interchanged looks, and afterward sir John found a softness in his fair one's manner, a languishing tenderness in her eyes, in the tone of her voice, and at the same time a modest perplexity and reserve about her, which altogether persuaded him that he was quite right, and his brother quite wrong *in fait d'amour*. Miss Flat appeared now to have the most self-possession of the three, and miss Sharperson looked at her, from time to time, as if she asked leave to be in love. Sir John's visit lasted a full half hour before he was sensible of having been five minutes engaged in this delightful conversation.

Miss Sharperson's coach now came to the door: he handed her into it, and she gave him a parting look, which satisfied him all was yet safe in her heart. Miss Flat, as he handed her into the carriage, said, 'Perhaps they should meet sir John at Tunbridge, where they were going in a few days.' She added some words, as she seated herself, which he scarcely noticed at the time, but they recurred afterwards disagreeably to his memory. The words were, 'I'm so glad we've a roomy coach, for of all things it annoys me to be *squeedged* in a carriage.'

This word *squeedged*, as he had not been used to it in Ireland, sounded to him extremely vulgar, and gave him suspicions of the most painful nature. He had the precaution, before he left Blackheath, to go into several shops, and to inquire something more concerning his fair ladies. All he heard was much to their advantage; that is, much to the advantage of miss Sharperson's fortune. All agreed that she was a rich Scotch heiress. A rich Scotch heiress, sir John wisely considered, might have an humble companion who spoke bad English. He concluded that *squeedged* was Scotch, blamed himself for his suspicions, and was more in love with his mistress and with himself than ever. As he returned to town, he framed the outline of a triumphant letter to his brother on his approaching marriage. The bet was a matter, at present, totally beneath his consideration. However, we must do him the justice to say, that like a man of honour he resolved that, as soon as he had won the lady's heart, he would *candidly* tell her his circumstances, and then leave her the choice either to marry him or break her heart, as she pleased. Just as he had formed this generous resolution, at a sudden turn of the road he overtook miss Sharperson's coach: he bowed and looked in as he passed, when, to his astonishment, he saw, *squeedged* up in the corner by miss Felicia, Mr Queasy. He thought that this was a blunder in etiquette that would never have been made in Ireland. Perhaps his mistress was of the same opinion, for she hastily pulled down the blind as sir John passed. A cold qualm came over the lover's heart. He lost no time in idle doubts and suspicions, but galloped on to town as fast as he could, and went immediately to call upon the Scotch officer with whom he had travelled, and whom he knew to be keen and prudent. He recollected the map of the Rascàlly estate, which he saw in miss Sharperson's breakfast-room, and he remembered that the lands were said to lie in that part of Scotland from which captain Murray came: from him he resolved to inquire into the state of the premises, before he should offer himself as tenant for life. Captain Murray assured him that there was no such place as Rascàlly in that part of Scotland; that he had never heard of any such person as miss Sharperson, though he was acquainted with every family and every estate in the neighbourhood where she fabled her's to be. O'Mooney drew, from memory, the map of the Rascàlly estate. Captain Murray examined the boundaries, and assured him that his cousin (the general's) lands joined his own at the very spot which he described, and that unless two straight lines could enclose a space, the Rascàlly estate could not be found.

Sir John, naturally of a warm temper, proceeded, however, with prudence. The Scotch officer admired his sagacity in detecting this adventurer. Sir John waited at his hotel for Queasy, who had promised to call to let him know when the ladies would go to Tunbridge. Queasy came. Nothing could equal his astonishment and dismay when he was told the news.

'No such place as the Rascàlly estate! Then I'm an undone man! an undone man!' cried poor Queasy, bursting into tears: 'but I'm certain it's impossible; and you'll find, sir John, you've been misinformed. I would stake my life upon it, miss Sharperson's a rich heiress, and has a rich grandmother. Why, she's five hundred pounds in my debt, and I know of her being thousands and thousands in the books of as good men as myself, to whom I've recommended her, which I wouldn't have done for my life if I had not known her to be solid. You'll find she'll prove a rich heiress, sir John.'

Sir John hoped so, but the proofs were not yet satisfactory. Queasy determined to inquire about her payments to certain creditors at Blackheath, and promised to give a decisive answer in the morning. O'Mooney saw that this man was too great a fool to be a knave; his perturbation was evidently the perturbation of a dupe, not of an accomplice: Queasy was made to 'be an anvil, not a hammer.'[238] In the midst of his own disappointment, our good-natured Hibernian really pitied this poor currier.

The next morning sir John went early to Blackheath. All was confusion at miss Sharperson's house; the steps covered with grates and furniture of all sorts; porters carrying out looking-glasses, Egyptian tables, and candelabras; the noise of workmen was heard in every apartment; and louder than all the rest, O'Mooney heard the curses that were denounced against his rich heiress – curses such as are bestowed on a swindler in the moment of detection by the tradesmen whom she has ruined.

Our hero, who was of a most happy temper, congratulated himself upon having, by his own wit and prudence, escaped making the practical bull of marrying a female swindler.

Now that Phelim's immediate hopes of marrying a rich heiress were over, his bet with his brother appeared to him of more consequence, and he rejoiced in the reflection that this was the third day he had spent in England, and that he had but once been detected. – The ides of March[239] were come, but not passed!

'My lads,' said he to the workmen who were busy in carrying out the furniture from miss Sharperson's house, 'all hands are at work, I see, in saving what they can from the wreck of *the Sharperson*. She was as well-fitted out a vessel, and in as gallant trim, as any ship upon the face of the earth.'

'Ship upon the face of the *yearth*!' repeated an English porter with a sneer; 'ship upon the face of the water, you should say, master; but I take it you be's an Irishman.'

O'Mooney had reason to be particularly vexed at being detected by this man, who spoke a miserable jargon, and who seemed not to have a very extensive range of ideas. He was one of those half-witted geniuses who catch at the shadow of an Irish bull. In fact, Phelim had merely made a lapsus linguæ,[240] and had used an expression justifiable by the authority of the elegant and witty lord Chesterfield,[241] who said – no, who *wrote* – that the English navy is the finest navy *upon the face of the earth*! But it was in vain for our hero to argue the point; he was detected – no matter how or by whom. But this was only his second detection, and three of his four days of probation were past.

He dined this day at captain Murray's. In the room in which they dined there was a picture of the captain, painted by Romney.[242] Sir John, who happened to be seated opposite to it, observed that it was a very fine picture; the more he looked at it the more he liked it. His admiration was at last unluckily expressed: he said, 'that's an incomparable, an inimitable picture; it is absolutely *more like than the original.*'*

A keen Scotch lady in company smiled, and repeated, '*More like than the original*! Sir John, if I had not been told by my relative here that you were an Englishman, I should have set you *doon*, from that speech, for an Irishman.'

---

* This bull was really made.

This unexpected detection brought the colour, for a moment, into sir John's face; but immediately recovering his presence of mind, he said, 'That was, I acknowledge, an excellent Irish bull; but in the course of my travels I have heard as good English bulls as Irish.'

To this captain Murray politely acceded, and he produced some laughable instances in support of the assertion, which gave the conversation a new turn.

O'Mooney felt extremely obliged to the captain for this, especially as he saw, by his countenance, that he also had suspicions of the truth. The first moment he found himself alone with Murray, our hero said to him, 'Murray, you are too good a fellow to impose upon, even in jest. Your keen countrywoman guessed the truth – I am an Irishman, but not a swindler. You shall hear why I conceal my country and name; only keep my secret till tomorrow night, or I shall lose a hundred guineas by my frankness.'

O'Mooney then explained to him the nature of his bet. 'This is only my third detection, and half of it voluntary, I might say, if I chose to higgle, which I scorn to do.'

Captain Murray was so much pleased by this openness, that as he shook hands with O'Mooney, he said, 'Give me leave to tell you, sir, that even if you should lose your bet by this frank behaviour, you will have gained a better thing – a friend.'

In the evening our hero went with his friend and a party of gentlemen to Maidenhead, near which place a battle was to be fought next day, between two famous pugilists, Bourke and Belcher.[243] At the appointed time the combatants appeared upon the stage; the whole boxing corps and the gentlemen *amateurs* crowded to behold the spectacle. Phelim O'Mooney's heart beat for the Irish champion Bourke; but he kept a guard upon his tongue, and had even the forbearance not to bet upon his countryman's head. How many rounds were fought, and how many minutes the fight lasted, how many blows were *put in* on each side, or which was the *game man* of the two, we forbear to decide or relate, as all this has been settled in the newspapers of the day; where also it was remarked, that Bourke, who lost the battle, 'was put into a post-chaise, and left *standing* half an hour, while another fight took place. This was very scandalous on the part of his friends,' says the humane newspaper historian, 'as the poor man might possibly be dying.'

Our hero O'Mooney's heart again got the better of his head. Forgetful of his bet, forgetful of every thing but humanity, he made his way up to the chaise, where Bourke was left. 'How are you my gay fellow?' said he. 'Can you *see at all with the eye that's knocked out?*'

The brutal populace, who overheard this question, set up a roar of laughter: 'A bull! a bull! an Irish bull! Did you hear the question this Irish gentleman asked his countryman?'

O'Mooney was detected a fourth time, and this time he was not ashamed. There was one man in the crowd who did not join in the laugh: a poor Irishman, of the name of Terence M'Dermod. He had in former times gone out a grousing, near Cork, with our hero; and the moment he heard his voice, he sprang forward, and with uncouth but honest demonstrations of joy, exclaimed, 'Ah, my dear master! my dear young master! Phelim O'Mooney, esq. And I have found your honour alive again? By the blessing of God above, I'll never part you now till I die; and I'll go to the world's end to sarve *yees*.'

O'Mooney wished him at the world's end this instant, yet could not prevail upon himself to check this affectionate follower of the O'Mooney's. He, however put half a crown into his hand, and hinted that if he wished really to serve him, it must be at some other time. The poor fellow threw down the money, saying, he would never leave him. 'Bid me do any thing, barring that. No, you shall never part me. Do what you plase with me, still I'll be close to your heart, like your own shadow: knock me down if you will, and wilcome, ten times a day, and I'll be up again like a ninepin: only let me sarve your honour; I'll ask no wages nor take none.'

There was no withstanding all this; and whether our hero's good-nature deceived him we shall not determine, but he thought it most prudent, as he could not get rid of Terence, to take him into his service, to let him into his secret, to make him swear that he would never utter the name of Phelim O'Mooney during the remainder of this day. Terence heard the secret of the bet with joy, entered into the jest with all the readiness of an Irishman, and with equal joy and readiness, swore by the hind leg of the holy lamb that he would never mention, even to his own dog, the name of Phelim O'Mooney, esq, good or bad, till past twelve o'clock; and further, that he would, till the clock should strike that hour, call his master sir John Bull, and nothing else, to all men, women, and children, upon the floor of God's creation.

Satisfied with the fulness of this oath, O'Mooney resolved to return to town with his man Terence M'Dermod. He, however, contrived, before he got there, to make a practical bull, by which he was detected a fifth time. He got into the coach which was driving *from* London instead of that which was driving *to* London, and he would have been carried rapidly to Oxford, had not his man Terence, after they had proceeded a mile and a half on the wrong road, put his head down from the top of the coach, crying, as he looked in at the window, 'Master, sir John Bull, are you there? Do you know we're in the wrong box, going to Oxford?'

'Your master's an Irishman, dare to say, as well as yourself,' said the coachman, as he let sir John out. He walked back to Maidenhead, and took a chaise to town.

It was six o'clock when he got to London, and he went into a coffee-house to dine. He sat down beside a gentleman who was reading the newspaper. 'Any news to-day, sir?'

The gentleman told him the news of the day, and then began to read aloud some paragraphs in a strong Hibernian accent. Our hero was sorry that he had met with another countryman; but he resolved to set a guard upon his lips, and he knew that his own accent could not betray him. The stranger read on till he came to a trial about a legacy which an old woman had left to her cats. O'Mooney exclaimed, 'I hate cats almost as much as old women; and if I had been the English minister, I would have laid the *dog-tax*[244] upon cats.'

'If you had been the *Irish* minister, you mean,' said the stranger, smiling; 'for I perceive now you are a countryman of my own.'

'How can you think so, sir?' said O'Mooney: 'You have no reason to suppose so from my accent, I believe.'

'None in life – quite the contrary; for you speak remarkable pure English – not the least note or half note of the brogue; but there's another sort of freemason sign by which we Hibernians know one another and are known all over the globe. Whether to call it a confusion of expressions or of ideas, I can't tell. Now an Englishman, if he had been saying what you did, sir, just now, would have taken time to separate the dog and the tax, and he would have put the tax upon cats, and let the dogs go about their own business.' Our hero, with his usual good-humour, acknowledged himself to be fairly detected.

'Well, sir,' said the stranger, 'if I had not found you out before by the blunder, I should be sure now you were my countryman by your good-humour. An Irishman can take what's said to him, provided no affront's meant, with more good-humour than any man on earth.'

'Ay, that he can,' cried O'Mooney: 'he lends himself, like the whale, to be tickled even by the fellow with the harpoon, till he finds what he is about, and then he pays away, and pitches the fellow, boat and all, to the devil.[245] Ah, countryman! you would give me credit indeed for my good humour if you knew what danger you have put me in by detecting me for an Irishman. I have been found out six times, and if I blunder twice more before twelve o'clock this night, I shall lose a hundred guineas by it: but I will make sure of my bet; for I will go home straight this minute, lock myself up in my room, and not say a word to any mortal till the watchman cries "past twelve o'clock," – then the fast and long lent of my tongue will be fairly over; and if you'll meet me, my dear friend, at the King's Arms, we will have a good supper and keep Easter for ever.'

Phelim, pursuant to his resolution, returned to his hotel, and shut himself up in his room, where he remained in perfect silence and consequent safety till about nine o'clock. Suddenly he heard a great huzzaing in the street; he looked out of the window, and saw that all the houses in the street were illuminated. His landlady came bustling into his apartment, followed by waiters and candles. His spirits instantly rose, though he did not clearly know the cause of the rejoicings. 'I give you joy, ma'am. What are you all illuminating for?' said he to his landlady.

Thank you, sir, with all my heart. I am not sure. It is either for a great victory or the peace. Bob – waiter – step out and inquire for the gentleman.

The gentleman preferred stepping out to inquire for himself. The illuminations were in honour of the peace.[246] He totally forgot his bet, his silence, and his prudence, in his sympathy with the general joy. He walked rapidly from street to street, admiring the various elegant devices. A crowd was standing before the windows of a house that was illuminated with extraordinary splendour. He inquired whose it was, and was informed that it belonged to a contractor, who had made an immense fortune by the war.

'Then I'm sure these illuminations of his for the peace are none of the most sincere,' said O'Mooney. The mob were of his opinion; and Phelim, who was now, alas! worked up to the proper pitch for blundering, added, by way of pleasing his audience still more – 'If this contractor had *illuminated* in character, it should have been with *dark lanterns.*'

'Should it? by Jasus! that would be an Irish illumination,' cried some one. 'Arrah, honey! you're an Irishman, whoever you are, and have spoke your mind in character.'

Sir John Bull was vexed that the piece of wit which he had aimed at the contractor had recoiled upon himself. 'It is always, as my countryman observed, by having too much wit that I blunder. The deuce take me if I sport a single bon mot more this night. This is only my seventh detection, I have an eighth blunder still *to the good*; and if I can but keep my wit to myself till I am out of purgatory, then I shall be in heaven, and may sing Io triumphe[247] in spite of my brother.'

Fortunately, Phelim had not made it any part of his bet that he should not speak to himself an Irish idiom, or that he should not *think* a bull. Resolved to be as obstinately silent as a monk of La Trappe,[248] he once more shut himself up in his cell, and fell fast asleep – dreamed that fat bulls of Basan[249] encompassed him round about – that he ran down a steep hill to escape them – that his foot slipped – he rolled to the bottom – felt the bull's horns in his side – heard the bull bellowing in his ears – wakened – and found Terence M'Dermod bellowing at his room door.

'Sir John Bull! sir John Bull! murder! murder! my dear master, sir John Bull! murder, robbery, and reward! let me in! for the love of the holy Virgin! they are all after you!'

'Who? are you drunk, Terence?' said sir John, opening the door.

'No, but they are mad – all mad.'

'Who?'

'The constable. They are all mad entirely, and the lord mayor, all along with your honour's making me swear I would not tell your name. Sure they are all coming armed in a body to put you in gaol for a forgery, unless I run back and tell them the truth – will I?'

'First tell me the truth, blunderer!'

'I'll make my affidavit I never blundered, plase your honour, but just went to the merchant's, as you ordered, with the draught, signed with the name I swore not to utter till past twelve. I presents the draught, and waits to be paid. "Are you Mr O'Mooney's servant?" says one of the clerks after a while. "No, sir, not at all, sir," said I; "I'm sir John Bull's at your sarvice." He puzzles and puzzles, and asks me did I bring the draught, and was that your writing at the bottom of it? I still said it was my master's writing, *sir John Bull's* and no other. They whispered from one up to t'other, and then said it was a forgery, as I overheard, and must go before the mayor. With that, while the master, who was called down to be examined as to his opinion, was putting on his glasses to spell it out, I gives them, one and all, the slip, and whips out of the street door and home to give your honour notice, and have been breaking my heart at the door this half hour to make you hear – and now you have it all.'

'I am in a worse dilemma now than when between the horns of the bull,' thought sir John: 'I must now either tell my real name, avow myself an Irishman, and so lose my bet, or else go to gaol.'

He preferred going to gaol. He resolved to pretend to be dumb, and he charged Terence not to betray him. The officers of justice came to take him up: sir John resigned himself to them, making signs that he could not speak. He was carried before a magistrate. The merchant had never seen Mr Phelim O'Mooney, but could swear to his handwriting and signature, having many of his letters and draughts. The draught in question was produced. Sir John Bull would neither acknowledge nor deny the signature, but in dumb show made signs of innocence. No art or persuasion could make him speak; he kept his fingers on his lips. One of the bailiffs offered to open sir John's mouth. Sir John clenched his hand, in token that if they used violence he knew his remedy. To the magistrate he was all bows and respect: but the law, in spite of civility, must take its course.

Terence M'Dermod beat his breast, and called upon all the saints in the Irish calendar when he saw the committal actually made out, and his dear master given over to the constables. Nothing but his own oath and his master's commanding eye, which was fixed upon him at this instant, could have made him forbear to utter, what he had never in his life been before so strongly tempted to tell – the truth.

Determined to win his wager, our hero suffered himself to be carried to a lock-up house, and persisted in keeping silence till the clock struck twelve! Then the charm was broken, and he spoke. He began talking to himself, and singing as loud as he possibly could. The next morning Terence, who was no longer bound by his oath to conceal Phelim's name, hastened to his master's correspondent in town, told the whole story, and O'Mooney was liberated. Having won his bet by his wit and steadiness, he had now the prudence to give up these adventuring schemes, to which he had so nearly become a dupe; he returned immediately to Ireland to his brother, and determined to settle quietly to business. His good brother paid him the hundred guineas most joyfully, declaring that he had never spent a hundred guineas better in his life than in recovering a brother. Phelim had now conquered his foolish dislike to trade: his brother took him into partnership, and Phelim O'Mooney never relapsed into sir John Bull.

Conclusion

Unable any longer to support the tone of irony, we joyfully speak in our own characters, and explicitly declare our opinion, that the Irish are an ingenious, generous people; that the bulls and blunders of which they are accused are often imputable to their neighbours, or that they are justifiable by ancient precedents, or that they are produced by their habits of using figurative and witty language. By what their good-humour is produced we know not; but that it exists we are certain. In Ireland, the countenance and heart expand at the approach of wit and humour: the poorest labourer forgets his poverty and toil in the pleasure of enjoying a joke. Amongst all classes of the people, provided no malice is obviously meant, none is apprehended. That such is the character of the majority of the nation there cannot *to us* be a more convincing and satisfactory proof than the manner in which a late publication* was received in Ireland. The Irish were the first to laugh at the caricatura of their ancient foibles, and it was generally taken merely as good-humoured raillery, not as insulting satire. If gratitude for this generosity has now betrayed us unawares into the language of panegyric, we may hope for pardon from the liberal of both nations. Those who are thoroughly acquainted with Ireland will most readily acknowledge

* **Castle Rackrent.**[250]

the justice of our praises; those who are ignorant of the country will not, perhaps, be displeased to have their knowledge of the people of Ireland extended. Many foreign pictures of Irishmen are as grotesque and absurd as the Chinese pictures of lions: having never seen that animal, the Chinese can paint him only from the descriptions of voyagers, which are sometimes ignorantly, sometimes wantonly exaggerated.[251]

In M. de Voltaire's Age of Lewis the Fourteenth we find the following passage: – 'Some nations seem made to be subject to others. The English have always had over the Irish the superiority of genius, wealth, and arms. The *superiority which the whites have over the negroes.**

A note in a subsequent edition informs us, that the injurious expression –'*The superiority which the whites have over the negroes,*' was erased by M. de Voltaire; and his editor subjoins his own opinion. The nearly savage state in which Ireland was when she was conquered, her superstition, the oppression exercised by the English, the religious fanaticism which divides the Irish into two hostile nations, such were the causes which have held down this people in depression and weakness. Religious hatreds are appeased, and this country has recovered her liberty. The Irish no longer yield to the English, either in industry or in information.'†

The last sentence of this note might, if it had reached the eyes or ears of the incensed Irish historian, Mr O'Halloran, have

---

* 'Il y a des nations don't l'une semble faite pour être soumise à l'autre. Les Anglois ont toujours eu sur les Irlandois la supériorité du génie, des richesses, et des armes. *La supériorité que les blancs ont sur les noirs.*[252]

† 'On lisait dans les premières éditions, *la supériorité que les blancs ont sur les négres.* M. de Voltaire effaca cette expression injurieuse. L'état presque sauvage ou étoit l'Irlande lorsqu'elle fut conquise, la superstition, l'oppression exercée par les Anglois, le fanatisme religieux qui divise les Irlandois en deux nations ennemies, telles sont les causes qui ont retenues ce peuple dans l'abaissement et dans foiblesse. Les haines religieuses se sont assoupies, et elle a repris sa liberté. *Les Irlandois ne le cédent plux aux Anglois ni en industrie ni en lumières.*'[253]

assuaged his wrath against Voltaire for the unguarded expression in the text; unless the amor patriæ of the historian, like the amour propre of some individuals, instead of being gratified by congratulations on their improvement, should be intent upon demonstrating that there never was any thing to improve. As we were neither *born nor bred* in Ireland, we cannot be supposed to possess this amor patriæ in its full force: we profess to be attached to the country only for its merits; we acknowledge that it is a matter of indifference to us whether the Irish derive their origin from the Spaniards, or the Milesians, or the Welsh: we are not so violently anxious as we ought to be to determine whether or not the language spoken by the Phœnician slave, in Terence's play, was Irish; nay, we should not break our hearts if it could never be satisfactorily proved that Albion is only another name for Ireland.* We moreover candidly confess that we are more interested in the fate of the present race of its inhabitants than in the historian of St Patrick, St Facharis, St Cormuc; the renowned Brien Boru; Tireldach, king of Connaught; M'Murrough, king of Leinster; Diarmod; Righ-Damnha; Labra-Loing-seach; Tighermas; Ollamh-Foldha; the M'Goilla-Phadraigs;[254] or even the great William of Ogham;[255] and by this declaration we have no fear of giving offence to any but rusty antiquaries. We think it somewhat more to the honour of Ireland to enumerate the names of some of the men of genius whom she has produced: Milton and Shakspeare stand unrivalled; but Ireland can boast of Usher, Boyle, Denham, Congreve, Molyneux, Farquhar, sir Richard Steele, Bickerstaff, sir Hans Sloane, Berkeley, Orrery, Parnel, Swift, T. Sheridan, Welsham, Bryan Robinson, Goldsmith, Sterne, Johnson,† Tickel, Brooke, Leland, Hussey Burgh, three Hamiltons, Young, Charlemont,

---

* See O'Halloran's History of Ireland.[256]
† Author of Chrysal, or Adventures of a Guinea.

Macklin, Murphy, Mrs Sheridan,* Francis Sheridan, Kirwan, Brinsley Sheridan, and Burke.[257]

We enter into no invidious comparisons: it is our sincere wish to conciliate both countries; and if in this slight essay we should succeed in diffusing a more just and enlarged idea of the Irish than has been generally entertained, we hope the English will deem it not an unacceptable service. Whatever might have been the policy of the English nation towards Ireland whilst she was a separate kingdom, since the union it can no longer be her wish to depreciate the talents or ridicule the language of Hibernians. One of the Czars of Russia used to take the cap and bells from his fool, and place it on the head of any of his subjects whom he wished to disgrace.[258] The idea of extending such a punishment to a whole nation was ingenious and magnanimous; but England cannot now put it into execution towards Ireland. Would it not be a practical bull to place the bells upon her own imperial head?

1801.

* Author of the beautiful moral tale Nourjahad.

Editors' Notes

1 'I can call spirits from the vasty deep'... 'But would they come when you did call on them?' Shakespeare, *1 Henry IV*, III.i.53.
2 Untraced. Perhaps intended as a summary of the quotation from *Measure to Measure* it leads into (see n. 3).
3 'Man, proud man/... like an angry ape/ Plays such fantastic tricks before high heaven/ As makes the angels weep; who, with our spleens,/ Would all themselves laugh mortal.' Isabella's plea to Angelo for her brother's life, *Measure for Measure*, II.ii.117–23. For the angels' competitiveness with man at the Creation, see text, p. 98, and n. 97 below.
4 Cf. 'Age cannot wither her, nor custom stale / Her infinite variety...' *Antony and Cleopatra*, II.ii.243.
5 John Locke (1632–1704), Edmund Burke (1729–97), Dugald Stewart (1753–1828), philosophical writers; as authorities, cited in a work about (alleged) national characteristics, it is important that they are, in turn, English, Irish and Scottish. Locke's phrase – 'wit lying most in the Assemblage of *Ideas*, and putting those together with Quickness and Variety' – is very close to the Edgeworths' formulation: see *An Essay Concerning Human Understanding*, 15th edn, vol. I (London: D. Browne et al., 1760), p. 117.
6 An anecdote likely to have been conveyed by someone with medical training, e.g. Maria Edgeworth's brother-in-law, Dr Thomas Beddoes of Bristol, or her half-brother Henry (b.1782), whose early education she supervised. In the late 1790s Henry began studying medicine at Edinburgh University, boarding with the moral philosopher Dugald Stewart (for whom see n. 5).
7 A famous couplet originating in a largely forgotten work. The Edgeworths give as the source Sir Richard Blackmore's Whiggish epic poem *Prince Arthur* (1695). In 1737 Matthew Green, quoting the same couplet in a footnote to his famous poem *The Spleen* (l. 24), more accurately traces it to another 12–canto

heroic poem set in the Dark Ages, *The Brittish Princes* [sic] (1669), by a Royalist, the Hon. Edward Howard. Howard's couplet reads: 'A Vest as Admir'd Vortiger had on,/Which from this Islands foes his Grandsire won.' (bk ii, canto 1; p. 96).

8 In alchemy, powder of projection was cast on to a metal in fusion to transmute it into gold.

9 As Killarney became (with the Giant's Causeway) one of Ireland's two major 18th-century tourist attractions, guidebooks proliferated which not only drew on local folklore, but padded out the notes with stereotypical jests such as Paddy Blake's. Irish journals such as the *Dublin Review* complain of stupidity and idle bookmaking in compilations such as R. Twiss, *Tour in Ireland* (1775; see n. 188 below), and John Carr, *Stranger in Ireland*, 1805. See Butler (ed.), *Castle Rackrent and Ennui*, 1992, Appendix, for the Edgeworths' involvement in one of these controversies.

10 French: Go away. Francis Bacon (1561–1626, Lord Verulam), *Sylva Sylvanum; or A Naturall Historie, in Ten Centuries* (London: William Lee, 1627), p. 67. The place is correctly Pont-Charenton.

11 Cf. 'The Chariot . . . undrawn, It self instinct with Spirit . . .' Milton, *Paradise Lost*, VI, l. 752. The OED notes that this usage (instinct, as adjective) was revived about 1800.

12 *Joe Miller's Jests* (1739) was named after a comic actor (1684–1738), and under different editorships kept in print well into the next century. In a footnote in 1802, 1803, afterwards cut, R. L. Edgeworth ('the eldest partner in the firm of this book') says he has 'read the whole of old *Joe Miller*, containing all the good things in about fifty jest books, published from 1558 to 1801'.

13 *c.* 356–324 BC, a close friend of Alexander the Great (356–323 BC).

14 The title of an episode in Cervantes's *Don Quixote*, one which provided a plot for several 17th-century English plays.

15 *Les Paroles remarquables, les bons mots, et les maximes des orientaux, traducion de leurs ouvrages en Arabe, en Persan, et en Turc, avec des remarques* (1694), p. 35. Galland (1646–1715) achieved celebrity from 1707 with his *Arabian Nights Entertainments*, which was rapidly translated into English.

16 'Towards the close of the reign of George II, the beautiful Countess of Coventry talking to him on shows, and thinking only of the figure she herself should make in the procession, told him the sight she most wished to see was a coronation.' *Walpoliana*, ed. J. Pinkerton, 2nd edn (London, 1800), vol. I, p. 1. But see n. 21.

17 Thomas Howard, 2nd Earl of Effingham said this to George III. *Letters of Horace Walpole: Fourth Earl of Orford*, ed. Paget Toynbee, 16 vols (Oxford: Clarendon, 1904–5), V, p. 122.

18 Henry IV of Navarre, King of France 1589–1610, the founder of the Bourbon line and often termed 'the Great', remained a hero to the English reading public as well as to the French, for the many shrewd, homely, common or provincial tales told of him and for his Protestant upbringing.

19 Madame Louise Denis (*c*.1710–90), niece and companion of Voltaire. Zara is *Zaïre*, tragedy by Voltaire (1732).

20 See Jean-François Marmontel, *Contes moraux* (Paris: Chez de Merlin Libraire, 1765), vol. II, p. 217.

21 [Horace Walpole (1717–97)], *Walpoliana*, ed. J.Pinkerton, 2 vols [1799], 2nd edn (1800), vol. I, p. 16. In 1791 Walpole became 4th Earl of Orford, a title more associated with his father, the Prime Minister Robert Walpole, whom George II made 1st Earl of Orford. This compilation by a Scottish antiquarian after H. Walpole's death contains some genuine, some spurious materials and was treated sceptically by discriminating readers. A Bodleian library copy, allegedly once the property of Edmund Malone, but acquired in the collection of the leading antiquarian Francis Douce, is prefaced by a warning [in Douce's hand?] that the 'jokes did not belong to Walpole but to Joe Miller.' 2nd edn [London: T. Bensley, 1800], front fly-leaf.

22 See *The History and Adventures of the Renowned Don Quixote*, trans. from the Spanish of Miguel de Cervantes Saavedra, *To which is prefixed, Some account of the Author's Life. By T. Smollett*, 2 vols (London: A. Millar, 1755) vol. II, bk ii, ch. 13, p. 185.

23 The immediate source for Molière's scene is the Roman writer Plautus (1st century BC). In Plautus's comedy *Amphitryo*, the god Mercury disguises himself as Sosias and then tries to persuade Sosias that he is not himself. The Edgeworths hypothesise a source in 'the Attic [i.e. Greek] Lucian', major prose writer of the silver age of Greek literature (*c*. AD 120 to 200), whose satires, dialogues and fantastic narratives draw on the manner and matter of two leading writers of classical ancient Athens – Plato (429–347 BC), author of witty philosophic dialogues, and Aristophanes, fifth-century BC comic dramatist.

24 Cf. Jean-Baptiste Pocquelin (1622–73), i.e. Molière, *Amphitrion, comédie*... *Amphitrion, a comedy* (London: John Watts, 1732), p. 40. The Edgeworths have compacted six of the original lines to produce their quoted three. The translation appears to be their own.

25 From John Burgoyne's *The Heiress; a Comedy in Five Acts* (1786), Act III, sc. ii.

26 Not traced.

27 Not traced.

28 Alexander Pope, 'Epistle I. To Sir Richard Temple, Lord Viscount Cobham' (1736), l. 88.

29 The Irish Lord Lieutenant was the King's representative; like the Viceroy, the title later used for India, he was effectively the Head of State within Ireland. The Council was his inner circle of senior advisers, using the name used in England for the (privy) council: in executive terms, the forerunner of the modern cabinet. In the last decade of Ireland's independent Parliament, the 1790s, Ireland was widely thought to be run by a trio who made up the core of the Council – John Foster, Speaker of the Irish House of Commons, John Beresford, Chief Commissioner of the Revenue and John Fitzgibbon, the Lord Chancellor. It is a prize achievement to catch them perpetrating a bull.

30 Samuel Johnson aroused similar ridicule when in his *Journey to the Western Isles* (1775), p. 11, he observed that the hedges were of stone; Boswell afterwards commented that this phrasing was 'ludicrous', but Johnson's modern editors observe that in hill country in England and Scotland [as in Ireland] dry-stone walls in effect serve as hedges, so that the objection is pedantic. (*Tour to the Hebrides*, 1785; Boswell: *Life of Johnson*, ed. G. Birkbeck Hill, rev. L. F. Powell, 6 vols (Oxford: Clarendon Press, 1934–64), vol. V, pp. 74–5).

31 Samuel Butler, *Hudibras*, ed. Zachary Grey, 2 vols (Cambridge, 1744). Many of Grey's annotations are given in the standard modern edition, by J. Wilders (Oxford: Clarendon Press, 1967).

32 Moses brought God's commandments down from Mount Sinai on two tablets of stone (Exodus 34: 28, 29). Afterwards he had wooden parts of the tabernacle and the ark of the covenant made of shittim wood, from the acacia tree (Exodus 36: 20 and 37: 1).

33 James Christie (1730–1803), London-based auctioneer from 1766, was succeeded in the business by his son James Christie the Younger (1773–1831), also an antiquarian.

34 The able French critic of the French Academy's *Dictionary* could have been the scholar charged from 1785 with making a new one, the Abbé André Morellet. He appears (as an Encyclopaedist) in the Paris scenes of Edgeworth's *Ormond*.

35 The dedication to *Hermes; Or a Philosophical Inquiry Concerning Language and Universal Grammar. By J. H.* (London: Woodfall, 1751) was signed James Harris (1709–80); its principal error was to describe the dedicatee as 'Lord High Chancellor of Great Britain' – that office pertaining to England only.

36 'I'll run into the danger to lose the apprehension', spoken by Heartwell, the central character: Congreve, *The Old Bachelor* (1693), Act III, sc. i, l. 85. Cf. Hester Lynch Piozzi, *British Synonymy*, 2 vols (London: G. G. & J. Robinson, 1794), vol. II, p. 59.

37 Elizabeth Carter (1717–1806), learned poet, critic, translator, friend of women writers and of Samuel Johnson. A rare addition to the 3rd edn, 1808.

38 The Roman emperor who drew stairs up after him.

39 See Roger L'Estrange (1616–1704). Dr William Fogarty, Irish physician to the paranoid deviser of conspiracy theories, Titus Oates (1649–1705), became implicated in an alleged Catholic plot to assassinate King Charles II after Oates forged treasonous letters apparently sent by his own associates to French or French-paid Jesuits. *Irish Bulls* incorrectly states Fogarty was accused of forgery. Fogarty and the others were arrested on 28 September 1678 and questioned by the (Privy) Council, forerunner to the Cabinet, on 30 September, with the King in the chair. In his defence Fogarty produced specimens of his own handwriting as a doctor, to show he had not written documents planning the murder of the King's most valuable supporter in Ireland, James Butler, 1st Duke of Ormonde. Roger L'Estrange was the brilliant Royalist journalist whose satirical pamphlets (e.g., 'Narrative of the Plot' and 'A Further Discoverie of the Plot', 1678, 3rd edns 1680) eventually succeeded in exposing Oates's lies, though not before 24 Catholic laymen and priests had gone to the scaffold.

40 Sci-fa = 'scire facias', that is, 'you are to know ...'; fi-fa = 'fiere facias', that is, 'cause it to be done ...'; qui-tam = 'qui tam pro domino rege', that is, 'who as well for the lord the king ...'.

41 A duel between John Hely-Hutchinson, Provost of Trinity College, Dublin, 1774–94 and a William Doyle. The Provost had gout and Doyle rheumatism and the latter was so ill he was obliged to lean upon a crutch. Both fired but neither was wounded. Wilmot Harrison, *Memorable Dublin Houses: A Handy Guide with Illustrated Anecdotes* (Dublin: W. Leckie & Co., 1890).

42 *Latin*: it is right to be taught even by an enemy. Ovid, *Metamorphoses* 4, 428 (Teubner, ed. W. S. Anderson, Leipzig, 1991).

43 Munich and the state of which it is capital, Bavaria, were much cited in British journals before and after 1800 because of the social reformer Benjamin Thompson, who was known in Munich by the title, Count Rumford, awarded him for establishing economical and effective workhouses for the poor. While in England between 1796 and 1801 Rumford published two volumes of essays on his institutions, which were mainly in Munich.

44 *French*: 'beyond what is required by the statutes: he justified his view by saying – where useless things are concerned, we need only what's necessary'.

45 Established in 1785 under presidency of Lord Charlemont. R. L. Edgeworth was among the earliest members.

46 The most sensational earthquake of recent times destroyed much of Lisbon on 1 November 1755 and the succeeding days; the antiquarian and

meteorological observer William Stukeley called it 'one of the most awful and tremendous calamaties that has ever happened in the world'. (*Philosophical Transactions of the Royal Society, from their commencement, 1665, to the year 1800*. Abridged, by Charles Hutton et al. (London: Baldwin, 1809), vol. XI (1756–63), p. 192.) It is possible, however, that the quotation relates to a careful report from Professor Winthrop of the New England earthquake of 18 November 1755 (XI, p. 62), which originally appeared as Article 1 of the 50th volume of the *Philosophical Transactions of the Royal Society* for 1756. Much of this year's *Transactions* is taken up with reports of lesser earthquakes, tremors and disturbances of the sea, reported in from many parts of the world, e.g. Cologne, Cornwall and Sumatra.

47 Henry Carey's 'To Mankind: An Ode' (1772?), xxi, ll. 124–5.

48 Irish pronunciation stressed the final syllable of the word. The 'united men' were members of the Society of United Irishmen (founded 1791), whose leaders were imprisoned and interrogated in 1798 and 1799.

49 No copy has yet been located of the so-called *Children's Dictionary*, apparently a satirical publication, like the *Children's Catechism* (Belfast, 1794), an imitation of typical French-Revolutionary propaganda, issued by the United Irish Circle. See Kevin Whelan, *The Tree of Liberty* (Cork: Cork University Press, 1996), p. 76. Sir John Birkenhead (1615–79) was an active Royalist propagandist, several times imprisoned under the Commonwealth but rewarded at Charles II's Restoration (1660) by being made 'surveyor to the imprimery', i.e. government censor of printing and publishing. His better-known successor in this office, Roger L'Estrange, later suggested borrowing the work of the leading Dissenting divine Richard Baxter to construct a similar glossary. 'Mr Baxter's Words will be as good as a Non-conformist's Dictionary to us; and assist the World toward the Understanding of the Holy Dialect... not as the Language Currant [*sic*] of the Nation, but only as a Privy Cypher of Intelligence betwixt themselves, and the Cant, or Jargon of the Party.' *The Casuist Uncas'd*, 2nd edn (1680), unpaginated. (See n. 39.)

50 Beffroy de Reigny also published throughout the 1790s under the homely pseudonym 'Cousin Jacques'; most of his other titles are comic, fantastic and Lucianic. *Dictionnaire neologique des hommes et des choses* is subtitled, *ou notice alphabetique des hommes de la Revolution*, vols 1–3, Paris [1800], indicating that it is the first instalment of a satire on revolutionists. No more volumes were published.

51 Principally referring to widespread insurrection in 1798, but also to the heightened tension of the 1790s, the political turmoil of the Union debates (1799–1800), and the brief recurrence of insurrection in 1803.

52 The lively *Memoirs* of Jean François Paul de Gondi, Cardinal de Retz, a leader of the Fronde rebellion (1648–53) were first published in Amsterdam in 1719, and translated into English in 1723. They remained in print for most of the 18th century outside France, because of the discreditable picture they gave of the French court and the quarrels among its leading figures during the minority of Louis XIV.

53 After a crushing defeat inflicted on 21 June 1798 at Vinegar Hill, County Wexford, on a Catholic peasant rebel army, the English General Gerard Lake, in command of a largely Protestant Yeomanry, scoured the country for suspected rebels, and when he caught them did summary justice. Lord Cornwallis, the newly-appointed Lord Lieutenant and Commander-in-Chief in Ireland, was shocked at the bloodlust he found in Dublin, particularly against the Wexford and Wicklow priests. He had no illusions about the cruelty and indiscipline shown by both the Protestant Yeomanry and many of the troops, or the harsh treatment of civilians permitted by Lake's rules of engagement. 'I am much afraid that any man in a brown coat who is found within several miles of the field of action is butchered without discrimination.' W. E. H. Lecky, *History of Ireland in the Eighteenth Century*, 5 vols (London, 1892), esp. vol. IV, p. 473 and vol. V, p. 9; Thomas Pakenham, *The Year of Liberty* (London: Hodder & Stoughton, 1969), passim.

54 The able but hardline lawyer and politician, John Fitzgibbon, Lord Chancellor and recently created Earl of Clare, stoutly defended tough use of the army and militia, in practice condoning summary justice and the use of torture to gain information. On 19 February 1798 in the Irish House of Lords he made a ferocious speech, immediately published, which in reply to Lord Moira's call for Catholic Emancipation set out the case-histories of recent sectarian murders of Protestants in the eastern and southern Irish countryside. On 23 March, after the arrest in Dublin of 16 suspected revolutionaries, Clare was threatened in the street by a hostile mob. 'Some 40 or 50 blackguards did follow me down Castle Hill; but as I never go out unarmed, on my facing them suddenly with a pistol in my hand, they retreated with precipitation.' Quoted Pakenham, *Year of Liberty*, p. 47.

55 John Wilkins (1614–72), Bishop of Chester, founding member of the Royal Society, published *The Discovery of a World in the Moone* in 1638. In addition to theological works, he showed a highly theoretical interest in language with *An Essay towards a real character and a philosophical language* (1688). After his death some of the adventurous short books which had made him eccentric or notorious were published together in 1707, including 'Mercury: or the Secret and Swift Messenger', about secret languages and codes; and 'Mathematical

Magick; or the Wonders that may be performed by Mechanical Geometry', in which the first part, 'Archimedes', treats basic mechanics, and the second part, 'Daedalus', after a chapter on submarines, explores the possibility of building a machine that will fly. For the latter, see especially pp. 112–29.

56 *French*: lack of talent and lack of experience. Marie de Rabutin-Chantal, Marquise de Sévigné (1626–96), writer of letters which became a model for French stylists.

57 Mrs Piozzi tells how Prince Gonzaga di Castiglione, on a visit to England, dined in company with Johnson at the house of a mutual friend and, 'thinking it was a polite as well as a gay thing to drink the Doctor's health with sure proof that he had read his works', called out his toast down the length of the table. *British Synonymy*, II, p. 358. See n. 36. *The Rambler* appeared between 1750 and 1752.

58 *French*: No, but it deserves to be. John Moore, *A View of Society and Manners in France, Switzerland and Germany*, 2 vols (1779), vol. I, p. 30. Moore (1729–1802), Scottish physician, travel-writer and novelist, charmed the Edgeworths by his ability to capture the idiom and personality of the people he met, especially the Marquis de Fontenelle, the speaker in this passage, whose affectations Maria Edgeworth later borrows for French society women such as Mme de P in *Leonora* and Mme de Coulanges in *Emilie de Coulanges*.

59 *Latin*: mere Irish person. A conventional term to distinguish the Gaelic population from the 'Old English', often referred to, when they opposed the Crown as 'degenerate English'. Sir John Davies (1569–1626), sent to Ireland by James I in 1604 as solicitor-general, reported back severely on the military and civil policy there of James's predecessors. On the civil side, Davies complained that English law with its benefits had not been extended to the majority of the population, the 'mere Irish' or 'Irishry': 'It is evident by all the records of this Kingdome, that only the English Colonies, and some few, Septs of the Irishry ... wer [*sic*] admitted to the benefit of protection of the Lawes of England; and that the Irish generally ... were so far out of the protection of the Lawe, as it was often adiudged no fellony to kill a meere Irish-man in time of peace.' *A Discoverie of the True Causes why Ireland was never entirely subdued, nor brought under Obedience of the Crowne of England, untill the beginning of his Majesties most happie reign* (London: Jaggard, 1612); ed. Alexander B. Grosart, *Davies's Prose Works*, 2 vols (privately printed, 1876), vol. I, pp. 62, 64.

60 The court of star chamber, a mediaeval body which dealt with breaches of the peace, became notorious under the Stuarts and was abolished in 1641; it became synonymous with arbitrary power exercised by the monarchy or state. 'Informers' were prominent in the trials of United Irishmen who gave (usually sold) information to the state against their associates.

61 L'Abbé Gabriel Girard (c.1677–1748), *Synonymes françois, leurs significations, et le choix qu'il en faut faire pour parler avec justesse* (1736).

62 Galland's *Les Mille et une nuits* appeared in Paris, 12 vols (1704–17), and initially in English as *Arabian Nights Entertainments*, 3 vols (1707). The genie who emerges from the bottle occurs in the adventures of Sindbad the Sailor.

63 Alpine area in Switzerland, where Cretinism, a combination of physical deformity (in the form of goitres) and idiocy, is endemic.

64 *OED* derives Cockney from cocken-ey or 'cock's egg', a small misshapen egg.

65 A volcano – thought extinct – near Naples in south-central Italy, the eruption of which in AD 79 engulfed Pompeii and Heraculaneum; Sir William Hamilton (1730–1803), ambassador to the court of Naples, made 22 ascents of the mountain and witnessed the eruptions of 1776–7. See his *Observations on Mount Vesuvius, Mount Etna, and other Volcanos in a Series of Letters addressed to the Royal Society* (London, 1772); and *Campi Phlegræi, Observations on the Volcanos of the Two Sicilies as they have been communicated to the Royal Society of London*, 2 vols (Naples, 1776).

66 Mrs Catherine Cappe, author of *An Account of Two Charity Schools for the Education of Girls* (York, 1800), wrote a letter dated 30 June 1801 and published in the *Monthly Magazine* 12 (1 August 1801), pp. 7–8, in which she limits herself to protesting against the practice of apprenticing young girls. Her book describes these girls destined for manual work as ignorant (p. 27), but does not give the story of the pig and the calf.

67 Piozzi, *British Synonymy*, vol. II, p. 256. In the story as she tells it, Johnson describes the girl as 'a milliner's prentice'.

68 The four provinces of Ireland include Munster (in the south), Connaught (or Connacht, in the west); the others are Leinster and Ulster.

69 *French*: 'a very coarse blunder'. Armand Jean du Plessis, Cardinal de Richelieu (1585–1642) mistook one term of the name: Terentianus Maurus (the usual form, he flourished in the late 2nd century AD), for the adjectival form of Terence (Publius Terentius Afer, born c.190 BC, Latin dramatist).

70 The Edgeworths misread the eminent French humanist scholar variously known as Guillaume/Guilelmus Budé or Budaeus (1467–1540), who was sent a copy of More's *Utopia* (1516) by an English correspondent, and replied in Latin in a witty letter that he immediately published. Opening the topic of *Utopia*, Budé suavely falls in with the fiction's pretences – 'the island ... is said, by a singularly wonderful stroke of fortune (if we are to believe the story) ... to have kept [the true wisdom of Christianity] uncorrupted to this day'. Budé then approvingly summarises the leading principles the islanders

subscribe to, namely communitarianism, peace and contempt of gold and silver, and wishes that states calling themselves Christian had been equally ethical. Budé to Thomas Lupset, dated Paris, July 31st, 1st Latin edn, Paris 1517; eds Edward Surtz, SJ and J. H. Hexter, *Complete Works of St Thomas More* [with facing page translation] (New Haven: Yale University Press, 1965), vol. IV, p. 11, ll. 4–33.

71 In 1802, 1803, it is more clearly stated that Pope mistakes Decade the 8th, Novel the Ninth for the two months. Warburton's edition was published 1751.

72 An anecdote elsewhere attributed to the early 18th-century Duchess of Bolton, a natural daughter of the Duke of Monmouth, who amused George I by pretending to make blunders. After seeing Colley Cibber's comedy, *Love's Last Shift* (first performed, 1695), she spoke of it to the King as 'La Derniere Chemise de l'amour'. *Walpoliana*, ed. J. Pinkerton, 2nd edn (London, 1800), I, l. 15.

73 Apparently a reference to John Lydgate (*c*.1370–*c*.1450), poet and Benedictine monk. Conceivably, however, R. L. Edgeworth remembered his actual schoolmaster, Lydiat, making this observation (see n. 74); i.e., the footnote could be an error by one of the authors.

74 A presumably fictitious name, to disguise an episode from R. L. Edgeworth's schooldays in which other names are also altered. In real life R. L. Edgeworth, aged eight, was sent to Dr Lydiat's school at Warwick, not in Wales; there he was bullied by other boys and teased for his smallness and Irish accent, until he was taught to use an English accent by a grandson of the architect Christopher Wren. In a separate episode while at the school, he was taken home for the holidays by a family called Dewes, whom he always remembered with gratitude. At 14, by now at school in Drogheda, Ireland, he escaped a whipping in the same manner as Little Dominick. See R. L. Edgeworth, *Memoirs*, 2 vols (1820), vol. 1, pp. 47–55, 65–6.

75 Welsh scholars stressed the continuity of their cultural traditions back to ancient and Biblical times, partly out of the need to preserve their language and identity against Henry VIII's Acts of Union (1536–7) and the Act of Uniformity, which for a while required all public worship to be in English. Two myths of origins were widely canvassed at this time: that Gomer, son of Japhet, son of Noah, was the father of the British or Celtic people; and that Welsh was one of the 72 languages spoken in the Tower of Babel. John Davies of Mallwyd, best Welsh lexicographer and grammarian of the early 17th century, upheld the first, as did English contemporaries such as Philip Sidney. The Edgeworths, unsympathetic to the Welsh gentry's pride in their genealogy, misrepresent the use of 'ap', meaning son of. It predates surnames, and should be followed by the father's Christian name.

76 A being (archaic, usually facetious). Cf. Samuel Butler's satirical introduction of his hero, Hudibras: 'A wight he was, whose very sight wou'd/ Entitle him, Mirror of Knighthood.' *Hudibras* (1663–8), vol. I, pp. 15–16. The Welsh pedant Owen ap Jones resembles Hudibras and his squire Ralpho, as these two fervent obscurantists are described in Canto I.

77 A strong dialect pronunciation of English as spoken in Ireland; the word probably comes from Gaelic, 'bróg', meaning a shoe, though this derivation is contested.

78 Plockit = blockhead; crammer = grammar.

79 Priscian was a celebrated Roman grammarian. 'To break Priscian's head' means to violate the rules of grammar.

80 'Royal Charlie's now awa/Safely owre the friendly main;/Mony a heart will break in twa/Should he ne'er come back again./Will you no come back again?/Will you no come back again?/Better lo'ed you'll never be,/And will you no come back again?' From the wellknown Jacobite song, referring to Prince Charles Edward's escape from Skye after his defeat at Culloden in 1745. In 1803 Owen ap Jones makes his exit saying, presumably in disapproval, – 'That is a scotch ballad, and the scotch are as bad as the Irish!' Similar songs conveying Jacobite sentiments occur in the Irish language after James II's flight into exile in 1690.

81 Harris, *Hermes; Or a Philosophical Inquiry Concerning Language and Universal Grammar*, first published in 1751.

82 Robert Lowth (1710–87), *A Short Introduction to English Grammar* (London: A. Millar; R. & J. Dodsley, 1762).

83 i.e. glibly.

84 Cf. Thomas Gray's 'Elegy Written in a Country Churchyard' (1751), l. 52.

85 A cluster of echoes of *Hamlet*: I.v.33 and 57, and II.ii.608.

86 Laurence Sterne (1713–68) and Jonathan Swift (1667–1745), both Irish-born, were among the great prose-writers in English and the great wits.

87 James Cook (1728–79), English navigator whose voyages of discovery to the South Pacific led to the British settlement of Australia from 1788.

88 Alexander Pope, 'The Dunciad' (1742), bk iv, ll. 31–4.

89 Charles Hutton (1737–1823), *A Treatise on Mensuration, both in Theory and Practice* (London: T. Saint, first published in 1770), p. 87. The John Machin (1679?-1751) referred to was fellow (1710) of the Royal Society and Professor of Astronomy at Gresham College, London (1713–51).

90 The fashionable world.

91 The authors attribute this advice to the *Letters to his Son* (1774) of Philip Dormer Stanhope (1694–1773), 4th earl of Chesterfield. It sounds like an inac-

curate recollection, perhaps the Edgeworths', of Pope's line from his portrait of Atticus (Addison): 'Willing to wound, and yet afraid to strike'. *Epistle to Dr Arbuthnot*, l. 203.

92 i.e. Midsummer Eve, a specially significant date for Catholic nationalist historians (e.g. Geoffrey Keating, Sylvester O'Halloran), because of its link with ancient worship of the sun. The persistence of bonfires on this night in Irish country festivals was used to uphold myths of origins in either Carthage, North Africa, or Phoenicia in Asia Minor. See nn. 252, 255.

93 *2 Henry VI*, II.i.124.

94 On 11 January 1749, a notice appeared in the *London General Advertiser*, announcing a new conjuror who would perform various feats at the Haymarket theatre, of which the most spectacular would be his entry, in full view of the spectators, into a quart wine bottle. A large crowd paid for tickets, and grew restive as the conjuror failed to appear. His name remained concealed, so that the Edgeworths' identification, if true, adds to the story. In the ensuing riot a lit candle was thrown, causing a melée in which the evening's takings disappeared, along with a fine sword belonging to a member of the audience, the Duke of Cumberland. The 'bottle conjuror' hoax generated newspaper and magazine coverage, satirical prints, pamphlets, theatrical burlesques and passing references to human ingenuity (and gullibility), well into the 19th century. John Theophilus Desaguliers (1683–1744) published his lectures on the *System of Experimental Philosophy*, 2 vols, in 1719.

95 Proverbially dull, stupid.

96 George Wade (1673–1748), Irish soldier whose successful campaign against the Scottish Jacobites involved the construction of military roads.

97 In Pierre Bayle's ironic review of learned commentary on the Creation, under 'Adam', in *Dictionnaire historique et critique*, 2 tom (in 4), (Rotterdam, 1697), he first discusses claims that Adam exhibits 'infused science' in all branches of human knowledge, which must derive from his Creator. Bayle goes on to describe how God silenced the angels when they spoke of Man with disdain, by asking first the angels, then Adam, to name the beasts, Adam, and finally God himself. Adam triumphs each time, emerging as the archetypal ingenious prankster and folk-hero. Bayle's *Dictionary*, 1st English trans., 4 vols (London, 1710), p. 79.

98 *French*: Some have raised and straightaway dealt with absurd questions: this, for instance: should one twice carry out the same mode of execution on a criminal who has revived after having his head cut off? Neither of the 'old French books' professedly consulted here has been traced. But the question was neither absurd nor obscure in England, where the death penalty was

usually administered by hanging, and in the 18th century a few hanged men had been revived by friends. Medical men, notably R. L. Edgeworth's friend Erasmus Darwin, were profoundly interested in the threshold of animal life and death. The issue was most closely associated with the work of the Italian, Galvani, the subject of a series of articles, which set out arresting features of his work, the study of electricity in the air (atmospheric electricity) and in the body (animal electricity). *Monthly Magazine* 12 (1 January 1802, pp. 503–6). Later in 1802 Galvani's nephew John Aldini was controversially allowed in the interests of science to try to revive by electric shock a criminal just hanged at Newgate. See Aldini, *Account of the Late Improvements in Galvanism* . . . with Appendix, containing the author's experiments on the body of a Malefactor executed at Newgate (London: Cuthell & Martin, Murray, 1803).

99 Ecclesiastes 1:8.

100 Thomas Gray, 'Ode on a Distant Prospect of Eton College', ll. 95–6.

101 An imitation of Irish pronunciation.

102 This paragraph echoes in several details the narrative of Thady Quirk in the opening pages of Maria Edgeworth's novel, *Castle Rackrent* (1800).

103 Town in County Cork, south-western Ireland.

104 Dialect [mis]pronunciation of Edgeworthstown, County Longford, formerly Mastrim, a midlands town renamed after the author's founding ancestors.

105 Irish cudgel made from the oak or blackthorn found in the village of Shillelagh in County Wicklow.

106 Widdrington was an English hero at the battle of Otterbourn (1388), won by the Scots. Having lost both legs in the battle, he fought on (according to tradition) 'upon his stumps', and was celebrated in the popular ballad 'Chevy Chase', also known as 'The Hunting of the Cheviot'. Joseph Addison famously praised this ballad as part of his effort to revive interest in the genre. (*Spectator*, nos 70, 74; 21, 25 May 1711.) But the rhyme with 'dumps' made the scene comic, and Butler borrowed it in 1663 for a mock-heroic battle, in which Hudibras is assisted by a fairground bear. Bruin 'yet falling fought,/ And being down, still laid about;/ As Widdrington, in doleful dumps,/ Is said to fight upon his stumps.' *Hudibras*, First Part, Canto III, 93–6.

107 Corneille, *Le Cid* (1637), Act III, sc. ii.

108 This Italian quotation, also used to illustrate inconsistency, and attributed to Berni, occurs in Kames's *Elements of Criticism*, 3rd edn (Edinburgh: Millar, 1775), vol. II, p. 338.

109 On 27 August 1799 a British expeditionary force of 10,000 men invaded Holland, now occupied by French-revolutionary armies: hence the use by

Ostend's commander of the revolutionary calendar for the month and year, the 6th from the calendar's adoption. The British were under the command of two outstanding Scottish officers who had previously served together in the West Indies and against the Irish rebels: General Sir Ralph Abercromby and Major-General John Moore. During September Abercromby's force fought its way along the beaches: in the key engagement on 2 October 1799, the battle of Bergen-op-Zee, Moore's brigade took many casualties and Moore himself was seriously wounded. When in Ireland the two British soldiers kept discipline among their own troops and publicly criticised the conduct of most units on the government side: e.g. Abercromby's statement on 26 February 1798, that the militia were more dangerous to their friends than their enemies. See nn. 53, 54 and 210.

110 Milton, 'Samson Agonistes', ll. 100–2.
111 'Cowards die many times before their deaths', *Julius Caesar*, II.ii.32.
112 Gray,'Ode on a Distant Prospect of Eton College', x, ll. 91–4. See n. 100.
113 Milton, *Paradise Lost*, bk ii, ll. 401–6.
114 Churlish critic of Isocrates, Plato and Homer in 4th century BC.
115 A slightly inaccurate translation from Cicero's original, which literally reads, 'It is easy, indeed, to criticise some glowing word, if I may use this expression, and to laugh at it when the passion of the moment has cooled.' M.Tullius Cicero, *Orator*, 27, Loeb trans. H. M. Hubbell (London and Cambridge, Mass., 1939).
116 Translated from the Greek: 'When a tragic actor at the Olympic games in Smyrna pointed to the ground as he uttered the words "O Zeus!", then raised his hands to heaven at the words "and Earth!", Polenos, presiding at the Games, expelled him from the contest, saying, "The fellow has committed a solecism with his hand."' Philostratus, *Lives of the Sophists*, I.541–2, Loeb trans. by W. C. Wright (London &: Cambridge Mass., 1952). Philostratus tells the anecdote to demonstrate the wit of the sophist Polenos.
117 William Wollaston, *The Religion of Nature Delineated* [1724], 5th edn (1738), p. 8. The third of Wollaston's propositions on the nature of an ethical choice.
118 See John Drinkwater, *A History of the Late Siege of Gibraltar* (London, 1785), pp. 150–1.
119 *History of the Life of Ayder Ali Khan or New Memoirs concerning the East Indies, with Historical Notes* by M.M.D.L.T. [Monsieur M. de la Tour] 2 vols (London: Joseph Johnson, 1784), vol.II, pp. 76–7, 80. The French author describes himself on the title-page as the 'General of 10,000 men in the army of the Mogol [*sic*] empire, and formerly commander-in-Chief of the Artillery of Ayder Ali, and of a Body of European Troops in the Service of that Nabob'. He

tells a fascinating story of service with Ayder or Haider Ali and his son Tippoo, sultans of Mysore, who fought the East India Company's troops in sporadic campaigns during the 1780s and 1790s.

120 Herodotus, *The Histories*, trans. Aubrey de Selincourt (London: Penguin, 1954), bk vii, p. 429. During the Persian Wars (490–479 BC), a crisis in Greek history, the Persian king Xerxes ordered advisers from two recently annexed nations, the Egyptians and the Phoenicians, to build him pontoon bridges across the Hellespont, so that his huge army could attack Athens and the neighbouring small Greek states. The storm which in 480 destroyed the bridge and many of the ships delayed him, but the Athenians perhaps got more propaganda value from Xerxes' behaviour afterwards in 'punishing' the sea, a story that tended to make the tyrant look ridiculous. Xerxes was also said to have beheaded his two bridge-builders.

121 Change Alley, London, afterwards the Stock Exchange, the scene in the 1720s of fraudulent floating of shares in the South Seas, with subsequent prosecutions and bankruptcies. The Stock-Exchange term 'bear' means someone who speculates for or produces a fall in the market. *OED* agrees that the expression may derive from a witty analogy with bear-hunters' practice of bargaining for the bear's skin before it was caught.

122 Since the 18th century the terms 'bull' and 'bear' have been broadly used on the Stock Exchange to describe (respectively) an optimist or pessimist in share dealing. *OED* mentions the practices of Canadian fur traders as a possible source for this use of 'bear', but like the Edgeworths has no explanation for 'bull', other than as a 'correlative': i.e., they sound a natural pair, because of the alliteration, the shortness of the words and the largeness of the animals.

123 Cleomenes I was a King of Sparta from about 520 BC to about 488 BC, and an able soldier who for a while enabled Sparta to dominate other Greek city-states. In bk vi of his *History* of the Graeco-Persian wars, Herodotus describes Cleomenes's anger that the islanders of Aegina had agreed to supply Darius, King of Persia, thus endangering the small Greek states. Cleomenes went to Aegina with the intention of punishing the islanders, but one of them, Ram son of Polycrites, defied him. On leaving, Cleomenes demanded to know his name and was given it. He replied, 'Very well, Master Ram, get your horns sheathed in metal. There's trouble coming.' Herodotus, *Histories*, bk vi, p. 376.

124 River in south-west France.

125 Greek orator and statesman, b. 384 BC (or 383), famous for his simple yet powerful speeches.

126 Francis Bacon (1561–1626, Lord Verulam), leading Renaissance thinker, but by profession a lawyer and courtier. In 1621 he pleaded guilty to charges of

corruption and neglect, and was deprived of his public offices. Hence Pope's line, 'The wisest, brightest, meanest of mankind'. (*Essay on Man*, Ep. IV, l. 281).

127 Bacon, 'Of Boldnesse', *Essays*, ed. Michael Kiernan (Oxford: Clarendon Press, 1985), p. 37.

128 To accept a challenge to a duel or to propose one.

129 Port in north Wales and main point of embarkation from England and Wales to Ireland.

130 Samuel Hood, afterwards first Viscount Hood (1724–1816), leading British admiral under Rodney during the American war (1775–82). Hood succeeded Rodney on his retirement from ill-health in 1781 and was created Baron Hood of Catherington in the Irish peerage, 1782.

131 The first paragraph of this chapter parodies an Appendix, 'Of Figures and Modes of Pure Syllogisms', in Kames, *Sketches of the History of Man*, 4 vols in 2 (Dublin: Williams, 1774), vol. IV, an attempt on Kames's part to make transparent Aristotle's *Analytics*, his major contribution in Logic: 'a syllogism is an argument ... consisting of three properties, the last of which, called the conclusion, is inferred from the two preceding, which are called the premises. The conclusion having two terms, a subject and a predicate, its predicate is called the major term and its subject the minor term.'

132 Meeting-place in Dublin for merchants to do business.

133 hook: to rob or steal small articles such as gems by cutting a hole in the window and fishing, with perhaps a stick, string, and a hook. Hook and snivey or (corruption, after 1800) hook'em snivey: a crook of thick iron wire in a wooden handle, used to lever the wooden bolts of doors from without. The meaning of snivey on its own now lost. (Eric Partridge, *Dictionary of Slang and Unconventional English*, ed. Patrick Beale, 8th edn (London: Routledge, 1984).) Though the authors provide an innocent meaning for this device, and it could have been used to position a coin, its normal user was evidently a thief.

134 Henry Home, Lord Kames, supported the authenticity of James Macpherson's translation of two epics published separately as quartos, *Fingal* (1761, dated 1762) and *Temora* (1763), allegedly the work of the 3rd-century Gaelic poet Ossian. Their most influential admirer, however, was Hugh Blair, Professor of Rhetoric and Belles Lettres at Edinburgh, whose lectures from the appearance of *Fingal* were published in the one-volume popular edition of the *Works of Ossian* (1765) as *A Critical Dissertation on the Poems of Ossian*, along with an Appendix authenticating the poem. The Appendix was superseded in 1773 but it had launched the vogue for Ossian on the Continent. Kames approvingly discusses Ossian's language in his *Sketches of the History of Man*, 2 vols (Edinburgh, 1774), not referring here to Blair.

135 Virgil, *Aeneid*, bk 10, l. 767.

136 John Horne Tooke (1736–1812), radical, politician and philologist, author of *The Diversions of Parley* (1786), a satirical and political treatise which wittily 'democratises' the English language by tracing the origins and often the meaning of words back to a few simple elements.

137 Greek athlete of the late 6th century BC, reputed to have carried a heifer through the stadium at Olympia and to have eaten the whole of it afterwards.

138 The reference is to Demetrius of Phalerum, *De Elecutio* (On Style), a Greek treatise of the early 4th century BC many times translated into Latin or modern European languages from about 1550 to 1900. Demetrius criticises the tendency of the elevated style to become frigid, illustrating his point from an unknown writer who describes the Cyclops casting a boulder after Odysseus' ship: 'when the boulder was in mid career goats were browsing on it'. Demetrius comments that 'the conceit is extravagant and impossible'. Ed. and trans. W. Rhys Roberts (Cambridge: Cambridge University Press, 1902), p. 125 (Ch. 1, sect. 115).

139 See J. Warton, *An Essay on the Writings and Genius of Pope* (London, 1756), sect. iv, 'Of the Rape of the Lock', p. 253n. Warton's comments refer to Pope, *Rape of the Lock*, III, ll. 128–78.

140 Virgil, *Aeneid*, bk 2, l. 553: bk 10, l. 536, conflated quote:

    2 l.553: extulit ac lateri capulo tenus abdidit ensem

    10 l.536: cervice orantis capulo tenus applicat ensem

141 As yet untraced.

142 'For true No-meaning puzzles more than Wit.' Pope, *Epistle II*: To a Lady. Of the Characters of Women' (1735), l.114.

143 See J. Ray, *A Collection of English Proverbs, Digested into a convenient Method for the speedy finding any one upon occasion; with short annotations. Whereunto are added Local Proverbs, with their Explications, Old Proverbial Rhythmes, Less Known or Exotick Sentences, and Scottish Proverbs* (Cambridge, 1670), pp. 195–6.

144 Market-town in south-east England near the coast of Kent.

145 George Lyttelton, 'Advice to a Lady' (1731), ll. 31–2: Nor make to dangerous wit a vain pretence, / But wisely rest content with modest sense.'

146 Thomas Fuller, *History of the Worthies of England* (1662), pt II, p. 65. Fuller puts another construction on the old man's terseness, that the witness is blamed for ignorance 'which is nothing but impatience in the Auditors unwilling to attend the end of the discourse.'

147 Sir Henry Fortescue, an English lawyer, served in Ireland as Lord Chief Justice of the Common Pleas, and was twice deputed by the Irish

Parliament to make representations in London concerning their grievances. The perception that the crime (and execution) rate was comparatively high in England was sustained through the 16th century, a point Irish spokesmen made use of. Cf. Kames, *Sketches of the History of Man* (1774), vol. I, p. 110.

148 Phineas Fletcher, 'Brittain's Ida' (1628), Canto V, l. 2. 'Yet never durst his faint and coward heart/ (Ah Foole! faint heart faire lady ne'er could win!)' Poem written in Spenserian manner, and asserted by its original printer, Thomas Walkley, to be Spenser's, though first published nearly three decades after his death. Hence the frequent appearance of this poem in editions of Spenser before the later 19th century.

149 Thomas Gray, 'Ode on a Distant Prospect of Eton College', l. 46.

150 'The old French officer . . . said "it was a bon mot – and as a bon mot is always worth something at Paris, he offered me a pinch of snuff." Laurence Sterne, *Sentimental Journey*, chapter entitled The Dwarf, Paris', ed. Gardner C. Stout (Berkeley: University of California Press, 1967), p. 179.

151 Cicero, *Pro Sestio*, xlv. 98. A well-known quotation for a desired condition, presumably associated with the aristocratic Fitzgerald family. A son of the first Duke of Leinster, Lord Edward Fitzgerald (1763–98) became a leading figure in the revolutionary secret society, the United Irishmen, was wounded while being arrested and sent to Newgate, where he died.

152 Expensive shopping street in central London.

153 Traditionally attributed to Sir Boyle Roche (1743–1807), Irish MP.

154 Variation on the Biblical phrase for common men, hewers of wood and drawers of water, Joshua 9: 21.

155 'cottiers' = cottagers; 'gossoons' = garçons, boys – translated in 1802 version.

156 *The Iliad of Homer*, trans. Alexander Pope, 6 vols (London, 1715), bk 16, ll. 954–5, p. 1255, Endnote.

157 Homer, *The Iliad*, bk ii, 470–4.

158 While Kames touches on the question of the low in his *Elements of Criticism*, 2 vols, 1762, e.g., vol. I, p. 220 and vol. II, p. 492, and on Homer elsewhere, *Irish Bulls*' summaries seem closer to James Beattie's remarks on this passage in his 'Essay on Laughter and Ludicrous Composition' in *Essays*, 2 vols (Edinburgh, 1776), vol. II.

159 Adam Smith, *Theory of Moral Sentiments* [1759], eds D. D. Raphael and A. L. McKie, *Glasgow Edition of Smith's Works* (Oxford: Oxford University Press, 1976), pt. I, iii, pp. 2, 3.

160 See William Robertson, *The History of Scotland, during the Reigns of Queen Mary and of King James VI*, 2 vols (London, 1759), l. 225.

161 R. L. Edgeworth unsuccessfully contested the Longford county seat in a by-election in February 1796; he made an arrangement which secured him the borough seat of St Johns Town, County Longford (west of Granard) in February 1798. The speech of the poor freeholder, named in the 1802 edition as a Mr O'Neill, derives from R. L. Edgeworth's canvass on one or other occasion. The scene between the widow and her landlord was also witnessed by R. L. Edgeworth as a magistrate. Typically he came home and re-enacted the speeches, which Maria Edgeworth noted down. See R. L. Edgeworth, *Memoirs*, vol. II [by Maria Edgeworth], pp. 336–8.

162 Unlike an English ditch, an Irish ditch has a back side raised up into a bank.

163 Established in 1710 in Dublin to encourage the development of linen manufacture throughout Ireland.

164 Last line in Alexander Pope's 'Epistle from "Eloisa to Abelard"', written 1716, published a year later in the *Works*.

165 Impelling me by legal pressure to pay.

166 Men who lease land and then sub-let it again for a higher rent, much hated in Ireland.

167 Subjected to progressive increases of rent; cf. *Castle Rackrent* where the verb is used to create a fictitious family name.

168 Literal translation of the Gaelic 'béal bocht', the Hiberno-English phrase connoting ostentatious complaint.

169 Prematurely born calf. The imputation may be of an unviable birth converted into what is now known as veal.

170 Logical argument in the form of three propositions, the last necessarily from the other two.

171 James Adams (1737–1802), Catholic divine and philologist interested in English, Latin and the Gaelic languages; a professor at the French Jesuit college at St Omer, where many Irish Catholic boys were educated. After the French Revolution he moved to Edinburgh; see n. 175.

172 'Shibboleth': a Hebrew word difficult to pronounce: hence said in the Bible (Judges, 12: 6) to have been used as a test for detecting foreigners and strangers.

173 Greeks spoke different regional dialects, but could understand one another. In literary language the dialect varied by convention: for the chorus in Greek tragedy (and pastoral poetry) Doric was always used, while Athenian tragedy, comedy (and prose literature) used Attic, the regional dialect of the region round Athens. Theophrastus (c.370–c.287 BC) lived at a time when Alexander's victories were spreading the use of Greek as a second language and thus probably hastening the decline of dialects.

174 Grammatical or syntactical errors or incongruities.

175 James Adams, *The Pronunciation of the English Language . . . with an Appendix on Dialect . . . and Vindication of the Dialect of Scotland* (Edinburgh, 1799), p. 157.

176 An adaptation of the line by Horace, 'Cupidum, pater optime, vires deficiunt.' *Latin*: That's what I'd like to do, revered Sir, but strength fails me. Horace was being urged by Trebonius to celebrate the victories of Octavius Caesar, later the emperor Augustus. Horace's shyness was tactical; by using the line, Adams indicated the pressure he was under to write in praise of Scotland. Horace, *Satires* II.i.12–13, trans. F. Muecke (1992).

177 William Dunbar (1465–1530?), leading poet using the Scots dialect; Gavin Douglas (1474?–1522), Bishop of Dunkeld, writer of allegorical poems, and translator into Scots of the *Aeneid*; Allan Ramsay (1686–1758), dialect poet and Jacobite; Robert Fergusson (1750–1774), dialect poet who inspired Burns; Robert Burns himself (1759–96), dialect poet and collector of Scots ballads and songs, who had a powerful original voice but also worked to recover a still-current Scots-language culture.

178 Adams, *Pronunciation of the English Language*, pp. 157–8.

179 Ibid., p. 160.

180 In 'An Essay on Laughter and Ludicrous Composition', Beattie makes three distinct points in a wider discussion of incongruity, which seem to have merged here: (1) Dryden, and other late 17th-century Court writers, affected a slangy language of the street (2) Dryden tastelessly employed this in translating part of the *Iliad* (3) the Scottish dialect of English sounds ludicrous and vulgar to fellow-Scots, and cannot appropriately be used for serious purposes. Beattie, *Essays*, vol. II, pp. 352–64.

181 Thady and Paddy, i.e. Thaddeus and Patrick, recur in popular literature and speech as typical Irish lower-class Christian names (cf. Thady Quirk in *Castle Rackrent*). Teague, another contraction of Thaddeus, and Pat are also used as stereotypes of vulgarity.

182 At the beginning of his *Histories*, Herodotus briefly refers to the dialects of particular groups, without, however, saying they could not make themselves understood to other Greeks. The use of different dialects in a single stage performance suggest otherwise. See n. 173.

183 John Vanbrugh and Colley Cibber, *The Provok'd Husband; or, a Journey to London* (London, 1725); and John O'Keeffe, *Wild Oats; or, The Strolling Gentleman*; a comedy in five acts (Dublin, 1790). Both were performed at the Theatre Royal, Covent Garden.

184 Former provinces in south and north-west France respectively.

185 Jean-Baptiste Pocquelin (1622–73), i.e. Molière, playwright; and Pierre Carlet de Chamblain de Marivaux (1688–1763), novelist and playwright.

186 From the dramatic dialogue, complete with glossary, by John Collier ('Tim Bobbin') entitled *A View of the Lancashire Dialect; by way of Dialogue; between Tummas o'Williams, o'Margit o'Roaf's, and Meary o'Dicks, o'Tummy o'Peggy's. Containing The Adventures and Misfortunes of a Lancashire Clown* [1746] (Leeds & Preston: J. & N. Binns, 1787), p. 23.

187 Perhaps a reference to Spenser's hostile descriptions of Irish rebels and outlaws, in e.g. *A New View of Ireland*; e.g. in *Faerie Queene*, bk v, where, imitating Homer, he compares the murmuring democratic mob to a swarm of insects (Canto II, xxxiii); or where, in keeping with Celtic folklore, he has the bandit Malengin turn rapidly into a succession of creatures to escape pursuit, a fox, a bush, a bird and a stone (Canto IX, xvii).

188 Richard Twiss (1747–1821), travel-writer; author of *A Tour in Ireland* (1776), an offensive survey that gave great offence in Dublin. In his amusing description of the *Tour's* reception, Joep Leerssen describes how chamberpots were manufactured with Twiss's portrait inside, to enable his Irish readers to relieve their feelings. (*Mere Irish and Fíor-Ghael: Studies in the Idea of Irish Nationality*, 2nd edn (Cork: Cork University Press, 1996), p. 355). The Edgeworths must have deplored Twiss's reliance on books by others, but they manage to mine his text for their own purposes. He describes Irish women dismissively, as neither attractive, educated or elegant, in his opening chapter on arrival. Near the end he quotes from a much earlier Scottish traveller, William Lithgow, a description of Yahoo-like Irishwomen with very long pendulous breasts, so long that they are able to give suck to babies strapped to their backs (pp. 155–6). Travelling from the Giant's Causeway to Killarney he has occasion to mention that port is very cheap (p. 100). The three points appear to have become fused.

189 'Oats. A grain, which in England is generally given to horses, but in Scotland supports the people.' Samuel Johnson, *Dictionary* (1755). 'Oats' was one of a cluster of definitions that made the Dictionary contentious, for reasons spelt out by Boswell: 'his introducing his own opinions, and even prejudices, under general definitions of words, while at the same time the original meaning of words is not explained, as his Tory, Whig, Pension, Oats, Excise and a few more, cannot be fully defended, and must be placed to his account of capricious and humorous indulgence.' *Life of Johnson* [1791], ed. G. Birkbeck Hill, vol. I, p. 294.

190 For Davies, see n. 59 above. The agriculturalist Arthur Young was admired for his *Tour* (1780) which describes conditions throughout Ireland in 1776–9 before Maria Edgeworth settled there.

191 'A hundred pistols would fly from their holsters' plays on Burke's celebrated eulogy of Marie Antoinette, 'I thought ten thousand swords must have leaped from their scabbards to avenge even a look that threatened her with insult. But the age of chivalry is gone.' *Reflections on the Revolution in France*, ed. C. C. O'Brien (London: Penguin, 1970), p. 170.

192 *The Government of the Tongue* (Oxford, At the Theater, 1674), written by the Author of *The Whole Duty of Man* [Richard Allestree?]. There were many editions, including at least five issues of an earlier one, from 1665, and further editions of the 1674 version to 1693. The authorship of this well-written tract against detraction and scoffing and in favour of charity has never been firmly established; Allestree, one contender, was a cleric of firm Anglican and Royalist sympathies, ousted from his living under the Commonwealth but a leading figure in Restoration Oxford. The spirit of the Edgeworths' summary of his sentiments, though not the exact words, are to be found in the 1665 edition, pp. 72–5 and 130.

193 Hirschau, village in the kingdom of Württemberg, known for its Benedictine monastery.

194 Two very different linguistic areas: the first is ostensibly that of the Jewish people, the language of the Old Testament; the second is an early Irish system of writing on stone by which the letters of the alphabet were represented by groups of line-incisions differentiated by number, length and relative position. But the two together suggest that the authors' target is Charles Vallency (1721–1812), whose 'worthless tracts on Irish philology' (*DNB*) drew on his theory of a Phoenician origin for the early inhabitants of Ireland. See n. 257 below.

195 *Macbeth*, IV.i.83.

196 Cicero (106–43 BC), great Roman orator; Earl of Chatham (1708–78), British statesman; Edmund Burke (1729–97), Dublin-born orator and political philosopher; Alexander Murray (1775–1813), self-taught multi-linguist.

197 'The eloquence of tears', phrase used by William Broome, a collaborator with others, including Pope, in translations of Homer and Virgil, in his 'On the Death of my Dear Friend, Mr. Elijah Fenton.' (1730), l. 85.

198 Voltaire, *Œdipe*, Act III, sc. i, l. 3.

199 Milton, *Samson Agonistes*, ll. 248–9.

200 Milton, *Paradise Lost*, bk ii, ll. 678–9.

201 Ibid., bk iv, ll. 323–4.

202 See Joseph Addison, A *Critique upon the Paradise Lost*, in *Paradise Lost. A Poem, in 12 Books.* By J. Milton (London, 1749), p. 8.

203 Ibid., p. 9.

204 See Hortensius, *Deinology: or, the Union of Reason and Elegance: being instructions to a young barrister, with a postscript, suggesting some considerations on the viva voce examination of witnesses at the English bar* (London, 1789), pp. 121f.

205 Ibid., p. 131.

206 Quoted in *Deinology*, but originally from Horace, *Satires* II.iii.248: 'Ludere par impar, equitare in harundine longa' (playing odd and even, riding horseback on a long stick).

207 As yet untraced.

208 *Julius Caesar*, II.i.324–6.

209 Corneille, *Le Cid*, II.ii.418.

210 William Pitt the Elder (1708–78) had a high public reputation as a patriot and orator, especially in the period of his ministry's victories over the French during the Seven Years War (1756–63). But cf. John Egmont, later 2nd Earl of Percival, who grumbles at his 'wonderful power of words, and a pompous diction, improved by the study of the poets, of rhetoric, the speeches of old orators ... [he cast] a glare about his absurd propositions which deceived ... the most numerous of his audience, but even triumphed over common sense within himself'. Quoted Jeremy Black, *Pitt the Elder* (Cambridge: Cambridge University Press, 1992), p. 133, from Egmont's unpublished pamphlet, BL Add.47012 B ff. 182–4.

211 On 8 March 1801 Sir Ralph Abercromby effected a landing in force in Aboukir Bay, Egypt, disembarking in a single day 14,000 infantry, 1,000 cavalry and 600 artillery; he had Moore with him once again, in command of the reserves. See n. 109. Their orders were to expel or capture the French army left there by Napoleon. At the battle for Alexandria on 21 March, Abercromby was fatally wounded. Moore's reserves, including the 28th foot and 42nd Highlanders, bore the brunt of the fighting, the Highlanders capturing the standard of Napoleon's 'invincibles'. Moore, though wounded, resumed command of the reserve at Cairo, where the French army surrendered.

212 'The gates of mercy shall be all shut up.' *Henry V*, III.iii.10.

213 Alexander Pope, 'An Essay on Criticism', ll. 130–1; cited by Kames, *Elements of Criticism*, II, p. 338.

214 *Latin*: who, though he [Caesar] himself was the only [true] emperor in the whole world the Roman people commanded, yet suffered me to be the second. *Irish Bulls* omits word me after qui. Cicero, *Pro Ligario*, in M. Tulli Ciceronis *Orationes*, II (ed. A. C. Clark, Oxford Classical Texts, 2nd edn, 1918); Loeb trans. N. H. Watts (Cambridge Mass. and London, 1953).

215 Oliver Goldsmith (1730?–94), 'Retaliation', ll. 35–6 and 41–2.

216 Published 1764.

217 Boswell describes how Johnson called in one morning to see Oliver Goldsmith, who had been arrested for not paying his rent. Johnson took a volume of the *Vicar of Wakefield* (pub. 1776) to the publisher's and sold it for 60 guineas, which he brought back to Goldsmith, enabling him to clear his debt. (See *Life of Johnson*, ed. Birkbeck Hill, vol. I, p. 415). Walpole's description of Goldsmith as 'an inspired idiot'is given in the editors' footnote here, quoting from Thomas Davies, *Memoirs of Garrick*, 2 vols (1780),vol. II, p. 151.

218 Robert Lloyd, 'Ode I' (1760?), l. 147 – 'Drive his light Courser'.

219. Edward Young, 'Satire V. On Women' (1728), ll. 399–400.

220 Samuel Johnson, 'London' (1738), ll. 87–8.

221 Richard Steele (1671–1729), Irish-born essayist.

222 Preface to his *Edition of Shakspear's Plays* (London, 1765), p. xii.

223 It was a common practice of caricaturists and print-makers to utilise a well-known image, e.g. the portrait of a popular hero such as Washington, for a portrait of a less familiar figure. We have not, however, identified the print of Louis XVI. The second example is a caricature by James Gillray, 'Shakespeare Sacrificed; or the Offering to Avarice', 20 June 1789, where the topic satirised is Alderman John Boydell's project of a 'Gallery' of illustrations to Shakespeare, specially commissioned from leading painters and engravers. It is one of these Shakespeare paintings that is travestied, Joshua Reynolds's histrionic 'Death of Cardinal Beaufort', illustrating 2 *Henry VI*, III.iii. For Reynolds's unintentionally comic demon, supporting the dying man's pillow, Gillray substitutes a larger, blacker Monster, peering centre-page through billowing smoke.

224 This curious story, apparently an urban myth, is widely found in the 19th century. It is a classic expression of popular irreverence towards the great, in this case the genius or a man of science.

225 Deal, town and port on south-east coast of England, thought to be the site where Julius Caesar landed in 55 BC.

226 John Foster (1740–1828), Baron Oriel, last Speaker of the Irish House of Commons, old schoolfellow of R. L. Edgeworth at Drogheda (see n. 74 above); one of the Irish political figures he most admired, despite Foster's opposition to Catholic emancipation.

227 M[onsieur] Egalité was Philippe, Duke of Orleans (b.1747), democratically minded cousin of King Louis XVI of France, who opposed Court policy during the Revolution, changed his name to Egalité on 11 September 1792, voted for the king's death in January 1793 and was himself guillotined on 6 November 1793. The Duke's pendulum clock would not presumably have

come on to the market before his death, one of several details fixing Phelim O'Mooney's adventures in the mid 1790s or later.

228 District of south-east London, once haunt of highwaymen.

229 The fast runner from a fairy tale is called Lightfoot. Cf. R. L. Edgeworth to Erasmus Darwin, 1790, *Memoirs*, II. 131: 'I am in the ridiculous situation of Lightfoot in the Fairy Tales who was obliged to tie his legs to restrain his speed!'.

230 i.e. an MP for one of the English counties. Known collectively as 'the knights of the shires', they were usually men of landed property, supported in their neighbourhood by other landowners, and to that extent speaking up for local interests in the capital. They enjoyed considerable social prestige in the country, and seldom shone as parliamentarians.

231 Expression untraced. The dearly bought hat recalls one bought by R. L. Edgeworth's courtier great-grandfather, Sir John, after he ran out of money on one of his trips to England. 'He actually sold the ground plot of a house in Dublin, to purchase a high crowned hat and feathers, which was then the mode.' R. L. Edgeworth, *Memoirs*, I. 11.

232 'without stint or stay', not sparing supply, e.g. of money or food to animals (stint); thus, avoiding any check to progress (stay). An expression used for travel, having the typical alliteration and succinctness of semi-proverbial folk expression. See n. 122.

233 Unidentified.

234 'Nil admirari' (*Latin*: to wonder at nothing). Advice associated with Chesterfield, *Letters to his Son*, 2 vols (1774), taken for a conduct-book in the cool aristocratic manner, and, in an increasingly middle-class ambience, widely criticised.

235 'Flat', slang for duffer or dupe.

236 A selection of various clichés used on departing, each expressive of distinct social attitudes.

237 'at a fault', a term from hunting with hounds, meaning to be checked by losing the scent; thus, metaphorically, to be puzzled what to do next.

238 'an anvil, not a hammer': metaphorically applied to Queasy, a man who is acted upon, not a man who acts. Pithy expression drawing on common life, semi-proverbial.

239 15th March. Cf. *Julius Caesar*, III.i.1, where Caesar chides the soothsayer who has predicted danger for this date.

240 *Latin*: slip of the tongue.

241 Like Johnson's use of hedges, Chesterfield's use of the earth extends to signify the surface of the globe, a common usage. See n. 30 and for Chesterfield nn. 91, 234.

242 George Romney (1734–1802), Lancashire painter of portraits and country scenes, using a direct accessible style admired by Maria Edgeworth.

243 Jem (James) Belcher (1781–1811) was the champion pugilist from 1799 to 1803. He defeated the Irish champion, Andrew Gamble, in five rounds on 22 December 1800 near Abershaw's gibbet on Wimbledon common, southwest of London, and Joe Bourke or Berks, not an Irishman, near Maidenhead on 25 November 1801. The two fights seem to be conflated in *Irish Bulls*. In this, the first mass spectator-sport, Belcher briefly made a great champion – a popular hero, loved not just for his courage and 'rapid dexterity', but for what the leading boxing writer Pierce Egan describes as his 'irresistible gaiety' (J. C. Reid, *Bucks and Bruisers: Pierce Egan and Regency England* (London: Routledge and Kegan Paul, 1971)), pp. 22, 132. Less is known about Bourke, except that he was taller and heavier than Belcher, and a butcher by trade. Pugilism or bare-knuckle fighting was a working-class sport, illegal from 1750 but patronised by royalty, and by the end of the 18th century an upper-class cult. Bouts took place in different country venues such as Maidenhead, nearly thirty miles up the Thames valley. Advertised usually by word of mouth, the best could still attract 30,000 spectators, mostly from the capital.

244 As part of many fiscal innovations to pay for the war with France, Pitt introduced a dog-tax in 1796 which, with a modification in 1808, survived at 12 shillings a year until 1866.

245 pay away, a nautical term normally used like paying out, for slackening a rope. But the speaker seems to envisage that the whale veers away, thus capsizing the boat with the harpoonist in it.

246 A truce between Britain and France after nine years of war was agreed and an outline signed by the British ambassador in Paris on 1 October 1801. Given that *Irish Bulls* was published the following April, it seems likely that it is the first signing, rather than the full-scale Peace of Amiens (March 1802), that features in Phelim's story.

247 The cry of triumph given by celebrants at ancient Greek festivals.

248 Soligny La Trappe is the site of the French abbey founded in 1140 where Trappist monks (called Cistercian monks from 1892) still live in extreme austerity and absolute silence.

249 'Many oxen are come about me; fat bulls of Basan close me in on every side.' 'As the hill of Basan, so is God's hill: even an high hill.' Psalms, 12, 11.

250 The Edgeworths had been nervous that in Ireland Maria Edgeworth's *Castle Rackrent* (1800) would be received as a satirical work, ridiculing Irish provinciality and backwardness. Their fears were not in fact wholly assuaged by its reception.

251 This well-known put-down of Chinese culture is of considerable antiquity; the assertion recurs in J. Barrow's *Travels to China*, 1804, a source much used by the Edgeworths in later books. The ignorant and wantonly exaggerated traveller to Ireland referred to would have been identified by many Irish readers as Richard Twiss, whose snobbery and habit of quoting absurd and very ancient travellers as authorities caused much resentment. See above, nn. 9, 188, and J. Leerssen, *Mere Irish and Fior-Ghael: Studies in the Idea of Irish Nationality . . . Prior to the Nineteenth Century* (Amsterdam: Benjamins, 1986), p. 360.

252 Voltaire, *Le Siècle de Louis XIV* [1751]; last sentence omitted in 'new corrected' edition (London: Dodsley, 1754), vol. I, p. 201. The context for Voltaire's remarks was the Irish Jacobite or Williamite war of 1788–91, in which Louis XIV as a Catholic fellow-monarch gave some support to James II. Voltaire's negative reaction to Ireland and the Irish was enforced by his dislike of religion.

253 The further corrected edition of Voltaire's *Louis XIV* referred to here appears from its last two sentences to date from the years of the Ascendancy Parliament, i.e. after 1782. In that case it had no chance of reaching in time 'the eyes or ears of the incensed Irish historian, Mr O'Halloran'. O'Halloran (1728–1807) initially made his name as a physician; his major historical works were published in the 1770s. The two earlier ones are the most defensive towards historians who have belittled Ireland, the Scotsmen Macpherson and Hume as well as Voltaire. See *Ierne Defended*, 1774, and *Introduction to the Study and History of the Antiquities of Ireland*, 1774.

254 The Edgeworths' list runs backward in time, so that the proper names become more fantastic and parodic; otherwise this gives an unkind but not altogether unfair impression of the opening sections in Sylvester O'Halloran, *General History of Ireland . . . to the close of the twelfth century*, 2 vols (London: Robinson, 1778), with its lists of names, genealogies and deaths, viz: Patrick (373–463), patron saint of Ireland; Facharis; Cormuc, or rather Cormac (836–908), king of Cashel and bishop (not a saint); Brien Boru, or more usually Brian Boru (926–1014), high king of Ireland who defeated the Danes; Tireldach, or probably Toirrdelbach ua Conchobair who invaded Munster in 1118, and became 'high king with opposition', died 1156; M'Murrough . . . Diarmod are the same person, i.e. Diarmait Mac Murchadha (d. 1171), king of Leinster traditionally held responsible for bringing the Anglo-Normans into Ireland; Righ-Damnha, or more correctly ríogh dámhna, chief poet(s); Labra-Loing-seach, or rather Labhraidh-Loinseach, known in English as Lowry the Mariner; Tighermas, or rather Tighear-mas, a culture king among

the Fomorian prehistoric/legendary occupants of Ireland; Ollamh-Foldha: the intended meaning is Poet(s) of Ireland, though the second word should be spelled Fodhla; the M'Goilla-Phadraigs, or rather the sept of Mac Giolla Pádraig.

255 William (d. 1349?), English Franciscan theologian and nominalist philosopher, generally known as William of Ockham (or Occam). The printer or author has accidentally or deliberately introduced a bull by substituting for the English place-name the Gaelic hybrid term 'ogham', used for an early Irish system of writing on stone by which the letters of the alphabet were represented by groups of line-incisions.

256 In the first book of his major work, the *General History* (1778), O'Halloran gives the myths of ancient origins, from Brutus (in Troy) or Mil (in Spain), much as they had been given by 17th-century Celticists and mythologists (pp. 1–15). He fully accepts the Carthaginian and Phoenician link: 'Phoenician history and ancient Irish is the same ... They both adored Bel, or the Sun, the moon and the stars ... The Carthaginians, who were confessedly a Phoenician colony, were, like the Irish, also called Poeni' (pp. 46–8). He accepts that Albion was a pre-Roman name for Britain (rather than for the English, as the English liked to believe) on p. 33, where he refers to 'the Albanian Irish'; he had previously discussed this in his *Introduction to a History* (1774), p. 198.

257 James Ussher [*sic*] (1580–1656), patristic scholar, ancient historian, generous Anglican colleague to Catholic scholars; the Hon. Robert Boyle (1626–91), scientist; Sir John Denham (1615–68), poet; William Congreve (1670–1729), dramatist; William Molyneux (1656–98), philosopher; George Farquhar (1678–1707), dramatist; Sir Richard Steele (1671–1729), politician and dramatist; Isaac Bickerstaff (1735–1812), dramatist and possibly criminal; Sir Hans Sloane (1660–1752), physician and – in effect – founder of the British Museum; George Berkeley (1684–1753), philosopher; Roger Boyle, Earl of Orrery (1621–79), soldier and dramatist; Thomas Parnell (1679–1717), poet; Jonathan Swift (1667–1745), greatest satirist in the language; Thomas Sheridan (1721–88), actor, lecturer on elocution and lexicographer; Richard Helsham [*sic*] (1682?–1738), natural philosopher; Bryan Robinson (1680–1754), physician and editor; Oliver Goldsmith (1728–74), poet and dramatist; Laurence Sterne (1713–68), novelist; Charles Johnstone [*sic*] (1719?–1800), barrister; Thomas Tickell [*sic*] (1686–1740), poet; Henry Brooke (1706–83), novelist and dramatist; Thomas Leland (1722–85), classicist and historian; Walter Hussey Burgh (1742–83), lawyer and Irish MP; three members of the Hamilton family, Jacobite exiles: Anthony Hamilton (1646–1720), soldier and author of the *Memoirs of the Comte du Grammont*; perhaps two of his brothers, George,

Richard and John, all three of whom also fought for James II, John dying at Aughrim (1691), last battle of the Irish Jacobite wars; Arthur Young (1741–1820), agriculturalist; James Caulfeild, Earl of Charlemont (1728–99), antiquarian and politician; Charles Macklin (1697?–1797), actor; Arthur Murphy (1730–1805), dramatist; Mrs Frances Sheridan (1724–66), novelist and miscellaneous writer; Charles Francis Sheridan (1750–1806), author, Irish politician; miscellaneous writer; Francis Sheridan (d.1844); Richard Kirwan (1753–1812), scientist; Richard Brinsley Sheridan (1751–1816), dramatist and politician; Edmund Burke (1730–97), political writer and parliamentary orator.

258 Czar Paul I (1754–1801), unstable son of the powerful Empress Catherine, succeeded to the throne in 1796 but pursued erratic foreign and military policies, partly because of his admiration for Bonaparte, while his behaviour at court was so offensive that he was rumoured to be insane. He was assassinated by a group of officers during the night of 23 March 1801.